LET'S TALK DEMENTIA
TAKE TWO

CAROL L. HOWELL

D1319886

Copyright 2021 Carol L. Howell
First edition – copyright 2021
All rights reserved. No part of this publication may be reproduced, stored in a retrieval system, or transmitted in any form or by any means – electronic, mechanical, photo-copying, recording, or otherwise – without the prior written permission of the author. The only exception is brief quotations in printed reviews. For information, email the author – carol@letstalkdementia.org.

ISBN – 9798777323620

This book does not contain medical advice. No changes in medication or care plan should be made without consulting a physician. The author is not a physician. The author disclaims liability for any medical outcomes that may occur as a result of applying the methods suggested in this book. SEEK THE ADVICE OF A PHYSICIAN BEFORE MAKING ANY CHANGES.

Scripture quotations are from the Holy Bible, New International Version, NIV. Copyright 1973, 1978, 1984, 2011 by Biblica, Inc. Used by permission of Zondervan. All rights reserved worldwide. www.zondervan.com. The "NIV" and "New International Version: are trademarks registered in the United States Patent and Trademark Office by Biblica, Inc.

This book is dedicated to the glory of God.
I pray He uses these pages to bless His children.

PREFACE

Thank you for picking this book for your next read. Time to read is a special time for me. I relax. I enter another person's story, and I enjoy that time so much. Maybe you are not feeling so relaxed at the moment. Maybe you are stressed about caregiving. Maybe you are afraid for your loved one's well-being. Well, you've come to the right place.

As you read, you will hear my Southern accent. Yes, I have one. I don't even try to hide it. It even comes through in my writing. I might use a phrase or two that makes you stop and pause, but that is a chance to add that phrase to your vocabulary. I offer them free of charge!

Know this. My goal is to help. My company, Let's Talk Dementia, is a faith-based non-profit, and our goal is to walk the journey of dementia with over-worked and under-appreciated caregivers. Our motto is, "Knowledge brings power. Power brings hope. Hope brings smiles!" Who doesn't need a few smiles? Check us out at www.letstalkdementia.org. You can email me at carol@letstalkdementia.org.

Blessings and smiles,

Carol Howell
Vera's daughter

INTRODUCTION
Not What I Expected

I am sitting at my desk beginning the process of writing another book. I've written several. Some of my books have been very successful, and some were written just for my own benefit. This book, I believe, will help caregivers who are struggling with the issues of dementia.

Before we get too far into this book, let me assure you of one thing. Life will NOT be what you are expecting. In fact, if you could just turn off the button labelled "what I expect," and push the button labelled "what I am not expecting," life might be easier. Dementia changes EVERYTHING. There is literally no part of the human experience that is unchanged when dementia enters the picture.

I know this. I know this well. My momma, Vera Jean Carpenter Pyatte Holder Feaster Holder, (and yes that was her actual name) was diagnosed with Alzheimer's type dementia in October of 2006. That day began my journey of learning about dementia, how to care for Momma, and trying to understand how MY world would change because of her diagnosis.

I had zero clue Momma would live 13 years with Alzheimer's. I had zero clue she would want me to take her story and share it with as many people as possible. I had zero clue she would make me laugh so hard I thought I would pee my pants, and I had zero clue I would cry my eyes out more times than I could count.

What I DID know was this – I wanted my Momma to know she

was loved. I wanted her diagnosis to make a difference in other people's lives, and I wanted her life to continue to matter long after her death. And it has. Momma passed on May 31, 2019 around 10:14 PM. If you knew my Momma, you can rest assured of several things. Let me enumerate them for you.

1. My Momma went straight to heaven on May 31st. She had experienced visions of Heaven before that day. I'll tell you about them in another chapter. I have such peace knowing she is experiencing life in a way I cannot imagine. I know she loved us all, but I also know she would not trade her life now for what she had on Earth. NO WAY!

2. My Momma left behind a family that will always be better because SHE was part of our world. My sisters, our families, Momma's friends and co-workers, myself, and even folks who were just acquaintances were better people because they met her.

3. My Momma is in Heaven decorating. I'm not entirely sure why Heaven would need a decorator, but Momma has her sewing machine going full speed making pillows, draperies, and maybe even clothing. She loved doing all that!

4. My Momma, if she had of realized this, would have waited until June 1, 2019 to pass away. By leaving this world with less than two hours left in the last day of the month, she was unable to keep the Social Security payment she received in May. She would NEVER have stood for this. If there was one thing my Momma loved, it was shopping, and she needed those checks to go shopping!

No, I am not being disrespectful. Momma truly loved to shop. She would have totally agreed with item #4!

While I am making a list, I think I will take a moment and try to list some of the things I would never have guessed when those fateful words "Mrs. Howell, your mother has dementia" came across my telephone.

1. I would never have guessed Momma would live 13 years with Alzheimer's. That is a long time to struggle with a fatal disease.

2. I would never have guessed Momma would greet everyone with "Hi, my name is Vera. I have Alzheimer's." She truly wanted everyone to know there was still LIFE in her, and she planned on living that life to its fullest. Now, if you were one of those people whom Momma might not have liked, she might say, "I've got Alzheimer's. What's YOUR problem?" OK, she could be snotty when she needed to, but she made us giggle the remainder of the time.

3. I would never have guessed Momma would be forced to move from one memory care to another because her long- term care policy had a glitch that changed her financial future in a huge way.

4. I would never have guessed Momma would be asked to leave the skilled nursing care community she resided in because SHE COULD WALK! Yes, they asked her to leave because SHE COULD WALK. That was not news to the staff, because Vera Holder WALKED into the community, and she walked everyday she lived there. After advising us that she needed to stay in her bed, and if she didn't, she would have to leave the community, I knew it was time to move her. After making plans to move her and advising the administrator of the pending move, he said, "Why are you doing that? We were willing to work with

her." Oh really? Let's see, the previous week he had called and advised we would need to hire a 24/7 private caregiver for Momma or she would need to move. Hmmmm, something was not adding up!

5. I would never have guessed Momma would spend her last days in a wonderful small group home where she entertained the staff.

6. I would never have guessed I would have slept on the floor of her room in that group home for twenty-four days.

7. I would never have guessed what her last moments on this earth would look like.

8. I would never have guessed Momma's diagnosis would lead to my non-profit, Let's Talk Dementia. This company is reaching individuals and helping caregivers in over 100 countries. All because of Momma.

9. I would never have guessed how God would bring about good through Momma's Alzheimer's journey.

No one wakes up one morning and says, "You know. I think it would be interesting to be a dementia caregiver. I bet it is a lot of fun." That is not a thought that crosses the mind of a person who has even an inkling of what dementia is. Yet, like you, becoming a dementia caregiver is exactly where I found myself. That journey became more complicated and concerning as the days went by, but the love we shared during those days can never be forgotten. This love also demanded to be verbalized and demonstrated to anyone and everyone who would give us a minute to share. The love we had for each other, and the love we had/have for The Lord were too important not to announce loudly!

This dementia caregiving journey is likely the hardest challenge you may have ever faced. Or maybe it isn't. Maybe you look back on life and find situations that were more challenging. If so, you are in a better position than I was. The thought of my Momma one day not recognizing me, not being able to talk, potentially losing her sight, not smiling at me... all these things tore me to pieces. It was only my faith (what small amounts I had) that brought me through with even a semblance of normalcy. On the other hand, "normalcy" is just a word. It is not a real thing. No one lives a "normal" life. No one escapes the challenges and trials of life. Normal? Who wants normal? Living on the edge while hanging on tightly to the unchanging hand of God is the best way to face life.

Hanging on to God's hand was something I thought I was good at. I had faced other life challenges, and I always "looked up." When Momma's needs increased, and her memory decreased, the life challenges became harder and more intense than any other life experience. However, not once did God wake up and say, "Good gracious. I had no clue Vera was doing so poorly. There is no way Carol is going to make it through this." NO SIREE! He did NOT say that. Instead, He said, "Carol Lynn, (He uses my middle name to get my attention – just like Momma used to do) my grace is sufficient. My strength is enough. My mercy is plentiful. My faithfulness never ends. I love you and your Momma more than you can begin to even think about. So, hold on to THAT."

And holding on is what I am still doing. Momma has been in Heaven over two years, and I think about her crazy little self all the time. I mean really – my mind seldom doesn't relate to Momma or a "Momma story" about 75 times a day. I don't mind that. I like having her in the forefront of my memory. I love playing videos of her singing, or telling a story, or making us giggle. This is the important part, I am so thrilled she is no longer suffering with Alzheimer's. Instead, she is in Heaven and happier than my mortal self can begin to comprehend. I don't want to comprehend that. I want to revel in knowing life is so much more. So much better. So much bigger. So much more colorful. So much more serene. And so FULL of JESUS.

As you continue to read the pages of this book, I hope you find comfort in the struggles we faced. I hope you get information that will help you if you face similar struggles. I hope, even more so, that you find JESUS to be as real for you as He was for Momma and still is for me.

Blessings and smiles,

Carol Howell

P.S. - I hope you previously read LET'S TALK DEMENTIA. It is an Amazon #1 Best Seller, and it goes into more detail about dementia and caregiving techniques. If you read it, you might notice some differences in information between that book and this one in regards to the science of Alzheimer's. As scientists have continued to discover more about Alzheimer's, the information has changed. We now know Alzheimer's is preventable, and there are many things that can be done to heal the brain. Therefore, information in this book offers more up-to-date information. There is hope for the future! As Dr. Daniel Amen says, "You are not stuck with the brain you have." [1] That is such great news.

CHAPTER 1
A Refresher Course

One shot in her back. Another shot in her back. The pain didn't subside, but the confusion was apparent. She insisted on more injections, and I refused to take her. It was the beginning of her dementia journey. I didn't know what was causing Momma's confusion, but I knew the injections seem to make things worse, and they were not helping her back pain. What I knew was something was not right. Something was changing the way Momma processed thought. She was having challenges on her job, getting lost around town, and having issues paying her bills.

Then the diagnosis came through. Dementia. My life changed that moment. I started down a road I had never traveled. I faced road signs and detours that were scary. I saw tall hills and narrow passages that brought tears and anxiety. How was I to make it through all of this? What is dementia? Is God paying attention?

> "Be strong and courageous. Do not be afraid. Do not be discouraged, for the Lord your God will be with you wherever you." (Joshua 1:9, NIV)

This is a refresher course for those of you who have read my book titled LET'S TALK DEMENTIA, or this is new information for those of you who need to order that book! (Nothing like blatant advertising! Go to www.letstalkdementia.org to place your order.

Dementia is the inability to think clearly which leads to difficulties with the activities of daily living.

What are the activities of daily living? I remember them by the acronym BEAD-T.
- Bathing
- Eating
- Ambulating
- Dressing
- Toileting

Let's look deeper into these five activities of daily living (also referred to as ADLs).

BATHING becomes a problem for individuals with dementia in several ways. They may think they have bathed when they have not. Therefore, they refuse to take another bath. They may think they have not bathed when they have, and they proceed to bathe two, three, or four times a day. They may also refuse to bathe entirely. The process is uncomfortable, embarrassing, and can even be painful as the disease causing their dementia advances.

EATING becomes a problem for individuals with dementia for many reasons. Alzheimer's causes an individual to lose their sense of smell. We eat with our nose before we eat with our mouth. When we smell chocolate chip cookies baking, our brain registers that info and sends it to the nose. The nose perks up and happiness registers in the brain. The brain then sends a signal to the belly that says, "wake up – cookies coming down the chute!"

With dementia, these processes stop happening. The disease causing the dementia is also causing malfunction in the brain. Whether the disease is Alzheimer's, Huntington's, Lewy Body, Picks, or a stroke, the brain is undergoing trauma. The brain is diseased.

The brain eventually will tell the person, "Don't eat. If you do, it will make you sick. Don't drink. If you do, it will make you really sick." Then the person ceases to eat and drink. The brain is sending wrong messages!

AMBULATING is the ability to move from point A to point B. Everyone moves about, even if they are wheelchair bound. This moving about becomes a problem when dementia enters the picture. For example, the brain must give all the signals and information to help an individual move from the chair to a standing position. They must stabilize themselves. They must discern which foot to move forward first and how to make that complete step occur. So many steps for a diseased brain.

DRESSING is an interesting ADL that becomes more of a problem for the caregiver than the individual with dementia. If you are like I was, it was VERY important Momma always looked her best. She insisted upon matching shirt and pants, earrings, bracelets, rings (on 6-8 fingers), makeup, and cologne, and this had to happen every day. If not, Momma would complain, but it really irked me.

I remember the first time I arrived to visit Momma and she did not have a bra on. I was mortified! What caregiver would ignore putting a bra on Momma. I was ready to hunt that caregiver down and give her a few words to think about. Then Momma said, "I don't want to wear my bra. It hurts." Oh, wait a minute. That was something I had not considered. The bras went away, and Momma was happier.

Dressing does become a problem when we try to force our desires on our folks with dementia. We don't want them wearing three sweaters in August, but they are cold. Therefore, we should back off and help pick sweaters that look good together. They might not want to wear pants that have zippers because they are not soft. Our response should be a quick trip to your favorite store to purchase pants that make them comfy and happy.

Dressing can be a problem, but it usually is not the worst problem in the caregiving story. (Unless they show up for Sunday

School wearing their bathing suit. OH MY!)

TOILETING is one of the biggest challenges in the activities of daily living. When our folks can no longer discern the need to potty, life changes course drastically and quickly. We take for granted the ability to know when we need to pee or poop. When that feeling no longer happens, when the brain no longer sends the signals, life becomes more complicated.

Let's take a moment and look at the beauty of disposable undergarments. I had a client call and ask when was a good time to begin using disposable undergarments with her loved one (ok, let's refer to our loved ones as "LO"). I asked if he was wetting himself or having a release of bowels that he could not control. She advised he was having some of these issues. I had an easy answer. "Now is the time to make the change." She was a little surprised, but I helped her see postponing the change would only make for more work. My client was concerned her LO would be offended by the suggestion of a "diaper." I assured her calling it a "diaper" was a very bad idea, but explaining the undergarments were just disposable underwear, and they would make him feel better, was the best approach. My advice was taken, and the transition was not a big deal.

There are over 200 types of dementia. They are brought on by different changes in the body, imbalances in the body, or various diseases. That means Alzheimer's and dementia are NOT the same thing. Let's look at that in review.

For ease of understanding, the simplest definition is: Alzheimer's is a disease of the brain. If you remember it in those terms, you will be more informed than 99% of the folks you come in contact with.

I could spend some time telling you about beta-amyloid plaque, tau, neurofibrillary tangles, neurons, etc., etc. However, let's keep things simple and easy to remember.

What happens to the brain when Alzheimer's has been diagnosed? Our brain is similar in appearance to a head of cauliflower. It has tight fitting pieces, folds, craters, and sections. The folds in the brain allow for more surface area. In fact, if the average brain were stretched out flat, it would cover an area between 20x11 inches and 20x23 inches in size. We require a large amount of brain tissue to retain the information needed to operate in our world.

The average weight of a human brain is 3 pounds. The female brain is usually smaller than a male brain. Before the men begin thinking too highly of themselves here, let me explain a possible reason for this fact. The female brain has craters and folds that are much deeper than the male brain. Therefore, the female brain is just more tightly packed.

When Alzheimer's begins, the first area it likes to attack is the HIPPOCAMPUS. The hippocampus is located in the medial temporal lobe. OK, let's make that simpler to remember. The temporal lobe is that area just above your ears. In many people, it is the location they most frequently experience headaches. If you were to drill a hole from one side of the head to the other, with the temporal lobe being your beginning point on the left and ending point on the right side of the head, the midway point would be the approximate location of the hippocampus.

The hippocampus is responsible for our ability to retain new information. Everything you have read thus far is finding a temporary home in your hippocampus. Think of it as a cardboard file box. This file box is a temporary storage place until we decide what to do with the files it contains. Thus, the hippocampus is a temporary storage facility until the information is distributed to another part of the brain to reside in a permanent file box.

When Alzheimer's enters the picture, the hippocampus is damaged and is no longer able to retain new information. It shrinks, holes develop, and it cannot hold on to new memories. Further, the memories cannot travel from the temporary file box of the hippocampus to a permanent file box somewhere else in the brain.

With Alzheimer's type dementia, the very first symptom is always short-term memory loss. It is called the "hallmark symptom," and it is often why doctors will diagnose someone with Alzheimer's before completing tests to rule out other types of dementia. We will discuss this in an upcoming chapter.

As the disease progresses, the brain actually begins to deteriorate, and holes develop. Picture that cauliflower I mentioned earlier. Now mentally take a knife and drill a hole into that cauliflower. That is much like what happens to the brain with dementia. These holes cause a world of problems for the individual with Alzheimer's.

Our memories, knowledge, intellect, likes, dislikes, bodily commands, etc., are housed within our brain. When holes develop in our brain, these things leave us. The information that was stored in that part of the brain is gone forever. This would explain why Alzheimer's patients forget loved ones, events, appointments, education, and on and on.

CHAPTER 2
Diagnosing Dementia

"Mrs. Howell, you mother has dementia." Those are words which shall forever be a part of my life. I was shocked. I was speechless. I felt sick. The information was given over the phone and came without any compassion or hope for the future.

Momma, on the other hand, was not upset when I told her what had been said. She knew her mother had Alzheimer's, and she knew she was experiencing problems. In her typical fashion, she assured me she would make it through this. She reminded me of the verse we held close to our heart.

"And we know that all things work together for good to them that love God, to them who are the called according to his purpose."
(Romans 8:28, KJV)

I am honored to receive phone calls from caregivers in several countries. Across the board, most caregivers have no clue the type of dementia their loved one has. How can this be? Did they not go to the doctor and inquire?

Caregivers often have NOT pursued a doctor's visit to discuss the dementia they are noticing in their loved one. The reasons are many.

- The loved one refuses to go
- The family things everything is OK and problems are just "old age"

- Caregivers do not want to know it is Alzheimer's as they feel that is a "death sentence"
- Lack of understanding that many dementias are curable

Whatever the reason, a doctor's visit, and complete testing is imperative. However, it consistently surprises me how many doctors will give the diagnosis of "Alzheimer's" by simply administering the MMSE – Mini Mental Status Exam. Let me tell you about this test.

The MMSE is a quick test that can be performed anywhere by anyone. The doctor might say to the individual –

- "I will tell you three words. Please remember those three words." The doctor will later ask the individual to recall those three words. Want to guess how often those words are recalled?
- "Who is the President?"
- "Where are you at this moment?"
- "What season of the year is this?"
- "I would like you to count backward from 100 by sevens." OK, dear reader, I challenge you to try this and see how far you get before using your fingers!
- "Repeat the phrase 'No ifs, ands or buts about it.'"
- "Take this paper in your right hand, fold it in half, and put it on the floor."
- "Please read this and do what it says." The paper might say "Close your eyes."
- "Make up and write a sentence about anything." Of course, we are hoping to see a complete sentence with a noun and a verb.
- A picture of a drawing is given to the individual with instructions to copy that picture on a blank piece of paper. The drawing is most usually two geometric designs that intersect.
- Now tell me the three words I asked you to remember

when we started this test.
- A piece of blank paper is given with instructions to
  - Draw a circle
    - Add the numbers 1 through 12, like on a clock
    - Draw the hands on the clock to show the time of 4:40.
- Now tell me the three words I asked you to remember when we started this test.

There is another test called "Short Blessed Test (SBT)." It looks like this –
- What year is it now?
- What month is it now?
- Please repeat this name and address after me –

John Brown, 42 Market Street, Chicago
John Brown, 42 Market Street, Chicago
John Brown, 42 Market Street, Chicago

Great, now remember that name and address for use in a few minutes.
- Without looking at your watch or the clock, tell me about what time you think it is.
- Count aloud backwards from 20 to 1
- Say the months of the year in reverse order. (Not as easy as you might think.)
- Repeat the name and address I asked you to remember earlier.

Both of these tests have scoring grids that help determine the level of cognition or lack thereof. Here is the important part, there are many factors in any given day that can affect the resulting score on these tests. Let's take a look at some of those factors.

- The individual is just having a yucky day. Feeling poorly, whether because of a physical or emotional or spiritual issue, can cause the brain to function less efficiently than it does on days when life is easy.

- Stress of being in the doctor's office is a big issue. There is a syndrome called "White Coat Syndrome." This occurs when individuals tense up when they go to the doctor. This happens in individuals who have absolutely zero cognitive issues as well as those who might have cognitive issues. For instance, blood pressure will often rise just because the doctor is in the room. This can lead to a prescription of blood pressure medication when the individual is really just stressed.

- On the opposite side of the above scenario, our loved ones might complete the tests with amazing ability, get in the car to go home, and have zero ability to re-call what just happened in the doctor's office. When this happens, doctors might assume the individual is just fine and ignore the reports from family or care-givers of the issues they are seeing. Don't let this happen. As a concerned caregiver, you must be ready to give detailed examples of times this individual has displayed cognitive deficiencies and how they affected life. I have spoken with several caregivers whose loved ones were able to study these tests, re-turn to the doctor and perform really well. I can-not explain to you how their brain was able to retain enough of the information to improve their success in scoring at a later time, but it does happen. The brain is incredible, and we will never figure it all out!

These are just a few examples, but it helps to explain why these tests should not be the only means used to diagnose someone with any specific type of dementia. The tests are certainly a great place to begin the process of diagnoses, but further testing needs to occur.

Time out for a personal example. I was in a car accident in 2019. My car was not cranked at the time of the accident, and I was hit from behind. (HOLD ON – "Cranked." What does it mean? I have come to learn that is a Southern Phrase. I thought everyone used that word. It means the ignition in my car was not on. I told you there were a few Southern phrases you would learn from this book!) I quickly realized I was not well. I was sent to a neurologist who was fantastic, and he was very interested in the work I do regarding dementia. He then said, "I am going to give you three words. I want you to remember them." I instantly knew he was administering a variation of the Mini Mental Status Exam. I became tense but determined to remember those three all-important words. Guess what. I did not remember them. I seriously failed the test. I could not name the presidents in reverse order (but I'm not sure I could have done that anyway), I could not count backwards by seven from 100, and those three elusive words were my breaking point. I cried. I hate to cry, but the tears just flowed. It was so disturbing. He diagnosed me with a concussion and ordered a comprehensive cognitive exam for a later date.

Upon beginning that comprehensive cognitive exam, the administrator said, I am going to give you three words to remember. I was so determined to remember those three words. Today I can tell you two of them were purple and giraffe. I said them over and over again in my head while he administered the exam. It was not an easy cognitive exam, and I was very stressed throughout it. However, my brain had begun to heal, and I passed with flying colors. AND I remembered those three words!

Back to diagnosing dementia. Bloodwork is among the first things to be checked. Is there an imbalance anywhere in the body that is causing cognitive deficiencies? An imbalance in Vitamin B, Vitamin D, thyroid hormones, C-reactive protein, among others needs to be addressed. Many imbalances in our body can cause dementia that is reversible.

Learning about day-to-day life is imperative. Is the person eating healthy foods each day, experiencing interaction with others, and finding ways to feel needed and useful in their life? Do they have issues with pain or discomfort resulting in changes in their daily activities? Are they drinking enough each day to remain hydrated? And, speaking of drinking, are they using alcoholic beverages throughout the day that could contribute to their cognitive issues? What about medications or drugs? Are they handled correctly, abused, or a problem? Are they visiting the bathroom regularly and successfully? In other words, are they constipated or having trouble eliminating from bowel or bladder?

A brain scan might be next on the list of tools used to make an accurate diagnosis. A scan will tell the doctor if the brain has experienced a stroke which resulted in vascular dementia. It can show shrinking of various areas of the brain, including the hippocampus. This shrinking of the hippocampus might lead to the diagnosis of Alzheimer's.

Scans can be used to detect changes in the blood vessels and other problems that might bring a diagnosis of hydrocephalus or subdural hematomas. Further, an EEG test can help a doctor learn if the person is having seizures, which might lead to dementia.

There is much information to be gained from scans of the brain. This information will lead to a more accurate diagnosis.

Why is this important? Great question. Let me explain with a simple example. If you were at the doctor for a cold, but he spent the entire time talking about your ingrown toenail and prescribing a cream for the nail, would you think that was strange? Of course, you would. "Hey, doc, how about let's talk about my runny nose and watery eyes!"

Yet, many doctors will automatically diagnose an individual

with Alzheimer's without asking the proper questions to make that diagnosis. DO NOT ALLOW THIS TO HAPPEN! If the words from the doctor's mouth are a diagnosis of any type of dementia BEFORE proper diagnostic testing has been completed, STOP THE TRUCK IMMEDIATELY. I mean that. Don't hesitate to tell the doctor you want more testing. You need to know WHY your loved one has dementia and what the name of the dementia is. This information will help you know if that dementia is (oh, please Lord) a reversible dementia. And if it is reversible, then let's reverse it and not assume it is Alzheimer's.

In my company, Let's Talk Dementia, I have been helping individuals for over 15 years. During that time, I have seen many cases of dementia other than Alzheimer's. In just a two-week period, recently, I had two advanced cases of Pick's Disease Dementia (also known as fronto-temporal lobe dementia) come across my desk. These families were dealing with cognitive issues that were much different than Alzheimer's, but the dementia was very real.

If your family doctor is not willing to order the needed tests for a complete and accurate diagnosis, ask to be referred to a neurologist who specializes in dementia. That is a great place to begin the journey of proper diagnosing of this life changing journey.

CHAPTER 3
We Have A Diagnosis... Now What?

Once the diagnosis is certain, and we know if the dementia is reversible or irreversible, plans must be made for the future. This is true for any disease/diagnosis we might receive. Understanding what the future "might" look like can bring about a degree of peace and empowerment. While it is absolutely true receiving a diagnosis of a disease that is incurable will never be good news, having a plan to move forward is helpful.

> "Because of the Lord's great love we are not consumed, for his compassions never fail. They are new every morning; great is your faithfulness. I say to myself, 'The Lord is my portion; therefore I will wait for him.'" (Lamentations 3:22-24 NIV)

On the opposite side of that empowerment, we must acknowledge the pain that comes with realizing our loved one may never get better. Their eventual decline is inevitable, and we might feel overwhelmed by this knowledge. Here are my thoughts.

I often hear individuals say, "Alzheimer's is just the worse disease ever!" I appreciate their pain. Obviously, they have walked through the tumultuous journey of Alzheimer's, and that process has forever changed them. I get it. I've done it! However, the caregivers who have loved and cared for someone with cancer, or severe burns, or a host of other diseases might not agree. I caution us to be aware of other's feelings when we proclaim our situation to be the worse thing possible. Until we have walked in the high-top sneakers of everyone in pain, we just don't know.

So, how do we move forward? You read books like this, listen to podcasts and watch videos and attend on-line seminars about dementia (please check out my resources at www.letstalkdementia.org – they are FREE!). You arm yourself with as much knowledge as possible to empower you to be the best caregiver possible. One other piece of advice – Don't believe everything you read about dementia on social media!

Will you become more successful in this caregiving journey? YES! Will you have a positive impact on your loved one with dementia? YES! Will you mess up? YES! Will you allow your mistakes to hinder your ability to move on and continue being the best caregiver possible? NO!

This statement is true – YOU ARE CAPABLE, AND YOU WILL MESS UP. You will look back on situations and wish you could redo those days, but here is a fact that is true in life. We cannot do everyday perfectly. Jesus Christ did, but you will never come close to that level of perfection. Thinking you might be perfect in this caregiving journey is just setting yourself up for failure. Friend, you've got enough stress without adding that bit of misconception to your world. Learn from mistakes, and move on. Then celebrate successes.

There are so many successes in the caregiving journey. Life is not ALL stress. Even though days are filled with hearing the same story 47 times, cleaning up a dirty bottom, making sure they don't wander, and preparing three meals and snacks and hydration each day, life with dementia has funny moments and inspiring moments and meaningful moments. Again, this is true no matter what life situation you might be facing.

One very important answer to the question "Now what?" is "remain calm." It is very important at this point to learn as much as you can about the diagnosis your loved one has received. The more you understand the type of dementia they have, the better prepared you will be for the future.

Don't give up. Now is not the time for your loved one to find a rocking chair and take up permanent residence. NO! Now is the time for them, and your entire household, to begin making life-style changes to fight the disease and reduce how quickly both the disease and the dementia progress. There is hope, and there are actions that need to be taken to make the future as bright and hopeful as possible.

Since my Momma's journey to Heaven, I have learned so much about preventing Alzheimer's. These action steps to prevent Alzheimer's also prove beneficial for the individual already diagnosed with the disease. This is especially true if they are in the beginning stages. However, and this is important, your brain can change. You can turn off bad genes you might have inherited. Think about that! Your brain can change. When my educational journey for dementia caregiving began, I was told the brain could not and did not change. We now know this is not true. The brain can heal and adapt. However, lifestyle changes must occur. Is it easy? No, but it is NOT hard. Is Alzheimer's de-mentia easy? No! That is why we must make the changes.

You might be wondering why the entire household should make changes. Statistically, the spouse of someone with Alzheimer's is 600 times more likely to develop the disease themselves. [2] Just because you might not see signs of decline within yourself or others in the home does not mean lifestyle changes can be delayed.

Let's look at this in a practical manner. We take our cars to the repair shop to have the oil changed and the tires rotated and whatever else we do to cars (I know very little about cars). We do not wait until everything falls apart to get it checked out. Likewise, we go to the doctor once a year for a wellness exam – blood pressure, bloodwork, mammogram, etc. This all makes sense. Making the necessary lifestyle changes now to prevent

Alzheimer's is the key. Here is why – ALZHEIMER'S IS PREVENT-ABLE!

Those words were not part of my vocabulary just a few short years ago. They are now very true, and these methods have been tested repeatedly. Let's start now with the changes you will make for everyone in your household. If you feel you cannot go "cold turkey" and do everything at once, then determine to make one change a week or one change a month. But don't delay it long. All the changes are cumulative, however we want the maximum benefit as early as possible. We want to heal our brains NOW.

Let me take a moment and clarify. These lifestyle changes will not cure Alzheimer's. They will, as proven repeatedly, slow the progression of the disease to such a point that life is better for a much greater period of time. This is great news.

CHAPTER 4
"Lifestyle Changes – Good Food"

As I think back about my Momma's journey with Alzheimer's, I can hear her saying, "Did I do anything to cause this?" I always told her no, but I now know her lifestyle choices had a great impact on her odds of getting Alzheimer's. If I had known that at the time, I still would have answered the same way. No one wants a "finger in the face" telling them everything is their fault. My sweet Momma would say, "If I can help just one person because of this disease, it will be worth it." And she is now helping folks in over 100 countries. Way to go Momma!

> "Therefore, if anyone is in Christ, the new creation
> has come: The old has gone, the new is here!"
> (2 Corinthians 5:17, NIV)

The hardest change to be made is diet. Most people would assume the hardest change would be exercise. Exercise is much easier once diet is under control. Let me get straight to what most folks find to be the most difficult lifestyle change – Changing to a plant-based diet.

Plant-based eating is so good. It is very tasty. It is easy. It is not expensive. It is incredibly healing. Most importantly, it is the way to change your body and your overall health. It will also change your brain, your belly, and your heart. You will see changes in blood pressure, blood sugar, inflammation levels, and a balance in vitamins and minerals.

I have spent my entire life fighting my weight. I have lost hundreds and hundreds of pounds, and I have gained hundreds and hundreds of pounds. My fat always came back! It was not until I learned about The Blue Zones that I realized the WHY of eating plant based. Let me explain.

For three years I was a strict vegan, and I gained weight. It takes special skill to gain weight as a vegan, but I was quite good at it. I gave up on being vegan, went back to eating the Standard American Diet (which is abbreviated SAD – and sad it truly is), saw my weight go up, again, and realized life had to change. Then I was introduced to The Blue Zones in Southwest Florida. Mr. David Longfield-Smith was the presenter of that information, and I was captivated. David changed my life, my health, and my future that day.

The Blue Zones are those five areas in the world where more individuals live to over 100 hundred years of age than any other parts of the world. Only one of those zones is in the United States, and it is located in Loma Linda, California. Mr. Dan Buettner traveled the world to visit these six areas, and he marked them on a map with a blue marker. Thus, they took on the name BLUE ZONES.

If you haven't purchased the Blue Zones cookbooks, do yourself the honor of owning one. From Mr. Buettner's latest cookbook, THE BLUE ZONES KITCHEN, I learned more about the eating habits of the folks in all of the Blue Zones. Basically, they all are plant-based eaters. Meat, when eaten, is a condiment, NOT an entrée or even a side dish. Some of the areas include fish. However, plants, nuts, seeds, and grains are the common foods in all these areas.

Fast forward a few months, and I picked up a book by Dr. David Perlmutter called THE GRAIN BRAIN WHOLE LIFE PLAN, and a book called THE ALZHEIMER'S SOLUTION, by Doctors Dean and Ayehsa Sherzai. I then attended a multi-week course by Dr. Daniel Amen. Every book I read and on-line course I viewed said the same thing. Plant-based eating changes the body. Plant-based eating changes the brain. Plant-based eating reduces the chances of getting Alzheimer's by as much as 95%. WHAT? I had never heard such information! More reading. More classes. Listening to more interviews with well-known researchers. Everyone was saying the same thing.

The Standard American Diet truly is SAD. It is addictive, and increases inflammation, and it is killing us. SAD? Yes, it truly is, but good news is coming. Hold on to your brussels sprouts!

Let's talk about inflammation for just a brief moment. I will discuss inflammation in more detail in chapter nine. Why do you care about inflammation? Inflammation is a necessity in the human body. When you cut your finger, inflammation occurs and the body sends healing to the finger. However, when the body stays in a constant state of inflammation, it leads to the major killers in our world – heart disease, diabetes, cancer, asthma and – Drum Roll, please – Alzheimer's. I was so surprised to learn that inflammation caused Alzheimer's, but it is 100% true. And what is the leading cause of inflammation in America? Sugar!

It is not surprising to know sugar is bad for folks with diabetes, but causing heart disease and Alzheimer's was big news. Here is another big piece of information. Since artificial sweeteners have been on the market, you would think diabetes statistics would show a decrease in the number of individuals with diabetes. The exact opposite is true. The artificial sweeteners are so harmful for the human body, and they are not lowering the blood sugar levels that need to be controlled. I was a huge user of Sweet-n-Low. Loved me some Sweet-n-Low in my coffee, tea, or anywhere else I could think to put it. Zero calories. That had to be good for reducing my waistline. Wrong answer. I lost zero weight while I was consuming this killer product.

Here I am today, plant-based eating, and happy. I have worked so hard to reduce my inflammation levels (as measured in blood-work by a HS-CRP test), and I will continue to reduce those levels. I am 14 pounds away from my goal weight. I've gone from a size 26 pants to a size 10, and I feel better. I have elim-inated gluten from my diet which also eliminated systemic itch-ing I had suffered with for ten years. I have experienced a huge decrease in anxiety and a huge increase in energy. Life is better when you eat clean.

So, what do I eat? No, I don't live off brussels sprouts and carrots. Yes, I eat those two great foods, but I roast them with a dash of olive oil and a generous dusting of nutritional yeast. (Nutri-tional yeast can be purchased at most grocery stores. It is an excellent parmesan cheese substitute and is EXTREMELY good for your body.) Most any veggie you can think of, I have cooked, and the only reject for me is beets. I wish I liked them, but YUCK! Just can't do it.

Breakfast might be chia pudding with fresh berries, walnuts and pumpkin seeds. Other mornings I have hot quinoa with almond milk, berries, walnuts and pumpkin seeds. And I add the sweet-ener I now know is not harmful. It is monk fruit. You can buy pure monk fruit, but it is often hard to find, and it doesn't measure like sugar. In addition, some brands of this super sweet product are not sweet at all. I have no clue what they do to make it "not sweet," but it happens. You can also buy monk fruit that has an added ingredient called "sugar." WHAT? They added sugar to monk fruit? Yes. To me it is like adding alcohol to a non-alcoholic beverage. Why would they do this? The answer, it sells!

It is important to remember we don't eat any artificial sweet-eners. The sweetener I use is Monk Fruit with erythritol. It is all natural and erythritol is a sugar alcohol. These two products together measure like sugar and taste like sugar, but there are zero calories and they don't raise blood sugar. Doctors Dean and Ayehsa Sherzai use monk fruit with erythritol in many recipes in their cookbook, THE 30-DAY ALZHEIMER'S SOLUTION – PREVENTING COGNITIVE DECLINE. Monk fruit with erythritol can be purchased pre-packaged at most grocery stores, but be sure to read the label. You only want those two ingredients. I purchase it in bulk form at my local Sprouts Grocery Store.

Breakfast most often is a green smoothie that is amazing. I recently purchased an online series by Dr. Brooke Goldner regarding her amazing healing from Lupus. Her story is incredible. Check it out at www.goodbyelupus.com. What caught my attention was her claim to heal diseases with supermarket foods. She was talking my language.

From that class I learned how to make hyper-nourishing smoothies, and my husband and I are having these smoothies for breakfast every day. Before I tell you how to make it, let me tell you the success we already have experienced.

My husband was recently diagnosed as diabetic. This was very disturbing to me. Individuals who are diabetic have a 50% increased chance of Alzheimer's. Back the truck up! That was not going to happen in my house! I am fighting back. As a result, I made the smoothie, asked him to taste it, and HE LIKED IT! Hallelujah!

After just ten days of drinking the smoothie each morning, his blood sugar dropped 10 points. We are now one month into this new way of eating, and his blood sugar stays in the 80s and low 90s when measured first thing each morning. That is a huge success! I am drinking the smoothies to lower my hs-C-Reactive Protein (the inflammation marker I mentioned earlier). In three months, we will both repeat blood work, so we can celebrate our successes.

The recipe I use is my own. I have played with several variations, and this recipe works best for both my husband and me.

Start with a high-powered blender. I love my VitaMix Blender. My VitaMix loves me! It is such a great addition to my kitchen. Fill the blender cannister with 8 ounces of fresh spinach, two carrots broken in half, one entire lemon (including the peel), ¼ cup whole flax seeds, 1 cup ice, 2 cups water, and 1 teaspoon Sweet Leaf Liquid Stevia. Blend until smooth. You might want to adjust how much stevia you use, according to taste.

If this recipe is too tart, use any fruit instead of the lemon. I recommend frozen bananas or frozen blueberries. In regards to the fruit in the smoothie, it will not raise your blood sugar. After attending Dr. Goldner's online seminar, I learned the WHY of blood sugar raising, and it has much more to do with animal fat than carbohydrates. So, enjoy the fruit in the smoothie. Dr. Goldner says, "Now the fruit is the 'spoonful of sugar to make the medicine go down,' to quote Mary Poppins, so I am not as concerned whether the fruit is frozen or fresh since we are using fruit for flavor and not to add to the total nutrient density."[3]

My recipe will fill you up and load you up with protein and greens and omega three in abundance. We are amazed everyday how much better we feel just with this change. Now remember, I had already been plant-based, but changing to these smoothies is bringing on better health and more energy. I am willing to bet your loved one with dementia will enjoy these smoothies, also.

Back to my daily food. Lunch at my house is the big meal of the day. This is totally because of lifestyle more than anything else. However, not eating anything 2-3 hours before bedtime does aid digestion, improve sleep, and helps the body process the food.

Our lunch is always at least one hot vegetable and a cold salad (think tossed salad or coleslaw or broccoli salad). I will add fish on special occasions, cauliflower pizza without cheese on Tuesday, and we have soup or chili or any of several other wonderful entrees. The food is really good, and my barbeque loving husband even enjoys it. I will admit he still eats barbeque every

Monday, but he does not eat meat the other six days. I'm willing to work with that.

Recipes for many of our favorite foods are included in this book. Keep reading!

Dinner is much lighter. My husband will have nuts, apple, and a muffin packed with Omega 3's. He may enjoy a healthy brownie made with sweet potatoes (recipe included in this book), or a tortilla with guacamole or humus.

For dinner I have a cooked veggie or a salad. You will think this is strange, but stick with me. One of my favorite desserts is peanut butter with ground flax seeds stirred in, add a little monk fruit with erythritol, and eat it as a dip with raw cauliflower. I'm telling you it is DELISH! I recently added chopped 100% cacao to the recipe. My taste buds did the happy dance!

All this talk about Omega 3s needs further explanation. Why are Omega 3s important? They reduce inflammation. Remember the leading cause of the main killers in our world? Answer – inflammation. I purchase flax seeds and chia seeds and grind them in my coffee grinder as I need them. Don't purchase pre-ground flax seeds or chia seeds. They are not as good for you and lose many health benefits. Once the ground seeds are exposed to air, they oxidize and are not as good for you. In addition, the seeds must be ground or soaked in water in order for the body to process the oils inside each seed. Otherwise, you pass them in your stool in the exact same form in which they were at the grocery store. The coffee grinder I like costs $16 on Amazon. (A great investment.) I then add the freshly ground seeds to most everything I cook. They go in coatings for vegetables or fish. They go in muffins and waffles and cookies. They go in smoothies and peanut butter. They go on Tuesday's pizza. If I can find a way to work them into a meal, I'm doing it. Omega 3s also- (according to www.facty.com[4])

- Fight depression and anxiety (and who among us is not dealing with anxiety?)
- Improve vision significantly
- Ensure healthy brain development in infants and fetuses
- Decrease chances of heart disease
- Prevent ADHD symptoms from manifesting in children
- Benefit individuals with metabolic syndrome
- Protect the body against inflammation
- Help to safeguard against autoimmune diseases
- Help with psychiatric disorders
- Help to slow down mental decline

Those are such good reasons to add these easy to use and inexpensive foods to your diet.

Dessert is now part of my world. I have spent years not eating dessert and begrudging those who indulged. Now I have peanut butter freezer balls or homemade gluten-free cookies. One a day, and that's it. I still have 14 pounds to lose. However, once those pounds hit the road, I might have two peanut butter freezer balls a day. Or not?? I have included the recipes for both these great desserts.

What we don't eat is anything preserved. Pretty much, if it comes in a box or a bag, has a label listing ingredients God did not make or I can't pronounce, I don't buy it. The only boxed item we eat is plant-based pasta. You can buy many plant-based pastas that are not 100% plants. Don't do that. Keep searching. I purchase my groceries from Aldi, and they sell lentil pasta that is 100% lentils and black bean pasta that is 100% black beans. I guarantee you will not tell a difference.

In regards to the much-loved American food – cheese – I have had a huge adjustment. Learning how cows are treated, how bad cow's milk is for us and, therefore their cheese, and learning from the top doctors and scientists about the detrimental effect on our body from cow's milk and cheese, I decided it was not for me. I don't eat it. Instead of cheese I use Nutritional Yeast on my veggies when I roast them. I scrap off the cheese on the frozen cauliflower crust pizza I buy and add Nutritional Yeast. It is so very good! You might want to try plant-based parmesan cheese. I purchase it at a store that sells healthy food in bulk. I scoop up a few pounds and keep it handy in my kitchen.

I think it is only fair to include recipes to help get you started. So here we go. (Some of these recipes are variations from THE BLUE ZONES COOKBOOK or THE 30-DAY ALZHEIMER'S SOLUTION – PREVENTING COGNITIVE DECLINE. Some of the recipes are my own creations.

BLUEBERRY DRESSING

1 cup fresh blueberries or frozen blueberries
¼ cup balsamic vinegar
3 tablespoons Monk Fruit with erythritol
1 Tablespoon lemon juice
Pinch of salt and pepper
1 Tablespoon olive oil (I use California Olive Oil)

Combine all ingredients in a blender. Continue blending until completely emulsified and creamy. This takes about 1 minute or so.

Refrigerate. It will go solid in the frig because of the oil. No problem. Place the container in a bowl of hot water, and it will dissolve and be ready in just a couple of minutes. See how many veggies you can put in that salad.

CREAMY AVOCADO CASHEW DRESSING

1 cup cashews
2 avocados
1 tablespoon parsley
3 cloves garlic
Juice of one lemon
Salt and pepper to taste

Throw all the ingredients in your high-powered blender. Blend until smooth.

LENTIL SOUP

½ cup vegetable broth
1 onion, chopped
2 carrots, peeled and chopped
4 garlic cloves, chopped
2 teaspoons ground cumin
1 teaspoon curry powder
½ teaspoon thyme
28 ounces diced tomatoes
1 cup lentils, rinsed, not cooked
4 cups vegetable broth
2 cups water
1 teaspoon salt
2 large handfuls of greens chopped small
1 or 2 tablespoons lemon juice
3 tablespoons freshly ground flax seeds

Warm the ½ cup vegetable broth in a large soup pot over medium heat. Add onion, carrots, and garlic. Cook about five minutes. Add seasonings and cook for about one minute. Add remaining ingredients. Raise heat and bring to a boil. Cover the pot, reduce the heat to simmer for 30-45 minutes, or until the lentils are tender. Transfer 2 cups to a blender and puree, and then add back to the soup. Or you can use immersion blender to puree a portion of the soup while it is in the pot.

DOUBLE BLACK CHILI

2 cans black beans, drained
1 can black eyed peas, drained
2 cans chopped tomatoes (I prefer the ones already seasoned)
32 ounces vegetable broth
1 medium onion chopped
½ cup chopped peppers
1 Tablespoon chili powder
1 Tablespoon ground cumin
1 teaspoon paprika
1 teaspoon garlic powder
3-4 BIG handfuls of spinach
2 Tablespoons nutritional yeast
3 Tablespoons freshly ground flax seeds

Mix together and simmer until all incorporated and wonderful.

WAFFLES

1 ¾ cup 100% whole wheat flour
2 tablespoons flaxseeds – whole
3 tablespoons water
1 ½ teaspoons baking powder
½ teaspoon ground turmeric
1 tablespoon vanilla extract
1 tablespoon cornstarch
¼ teaspoon salt
1/3 cup unsweetened applesauce
1 teaspoon apple cider vinegar
1 ¼ cups almond milk
¼ cup monk fruit with erythritol

Mix whole flaxseeds with water in a small bowl. Set aside. Combine the flours, baking powder, turmeric, vanilla, cornstarch, and salt in a large bowl. Gently stir in applesauce, apple cider vinegar, monk fruit, flaxseed mixture, and enough milk to get a thick batter. Do not overmix.

Spray the waffle iron and bake. Usually takes 2-3 minutes in small waffle iron. Be sure to spread the mixture over the entire waffle iron for prettier waffles.

LENTIL SLOPPY JOES

3 1/3 cups vegetable stock
1 onion, chopped
2 tablespoons chopped garlic
1 red bell pepper, chopped
2 tablespoons chili powder
1 tablespoon cumin
1 ½ cups dried brown or green lentils
1 - 15-ounce can diced fire-roasted tomatoes
3 tablespoons freshly ground flax seeds
2 tablespoons soy sauce
2 tablespoons Dijon mustard
1 tablespoon brown sugar
1 teaspoon balsamic vinegar
1 teaspoon Worcestershire sauce
Salt and pepper taste

Place 1 cup of stock in a large pot. Add the onions, garlic, and red pepper and cook, stirring occasionally until onions soften slightly, about 5 minutes. Add the chili powder, cumin, flax seeds and mix well. Add the remaining ingredients. Mix well, bring to a boil, reduce heat, cover and cook over low heat for one hour, stirring occasionally.

Serve on tortillas or lettuce cups.

CASHEW QUESO CHEESE

BY AYESHA SHERZAI[5]

1 ½ cups raw cashews
¼ cup nutritional yeast
½ teaspoon salt
¼ teaspoon garlic powder
1 cup boiling water
OPTIONAL -   ½ teaspoon cumin
              ¼ teaspoon chili powder

Add the cashews, nutritional yeast, salt and garlic powder to the blender on high speed. Blend, scraping the sides. Add small amounts of hot water through the top opening of the canister while the blender is running, and slowly blend until cheesy consistency. The author of this recipe, Dr. Ayesha Sherzai, includes 1 or 2 small chipotle peppers and the optional spices. I am not fond of hot foods, but do what makes your heart sing.

I use this cheese on everything Mexican or just the tip of my finger! Try it on raw veggies or cooked veggies. GOOD STUFF!

PLANT-BASED PEANUT BUTTER COOKIES

2 tablespoons applesauce
¾ cup Monk Fruit with Erythritol
½ cup peanut butter
2 tablespoons whole flax seeds
3 tablespoons water
2 tablespoons pumpkin pie spice
1 teaspoon pure vanilla extract
½ teaspoon baking soda
¼ teaspoon salt
2 cups almond flour (Not almond meal)
½ cup unsweetened shredded coconut

Preheat the oven to 350 degrees and line a baking sheet with parchment paper.

Mix whole flax seeds and water. Set aside for 10-15 minutes.

Mix applesauce, monk fruit, peanut butter, applesauce, pumpkin pie spice, baking soda, salt and vanilla in mixer. Add whole flax seed/water mixture. Add almond flour slowly. Pour into a big bowl and stir in coconut.

Make cookies about two tablespoons in size. Bake 10-12 minutes. You want the edges to get a bit brown. It makes about 2 dozen.

ROASTED VEGETABLES

This recipe works for ANY vegetable, including spinach and kale.

Preheat oven to 425 degrees. Cover baking pan with parchment paper.

Wash veggies. Slice thin. Toss with small amount of olive oil. Salt and pepper the vegetables. Add a layer of nutritional yeast and a sprinkling of freshly ground flax seeds.

Bake 20 minutes. If they are not as dark as you want, increase in two-minute increments.

BERRY CHIA PUDDING

2/3 cup chopped berries of your choice
1 tablespoon lemon juice
1 scoop Raspberry Powder (Order this from Amazon. It is SO GOOD FOR YOU but not essential for the recipe.)
1 ½ cups almond milk
½ cup monk fruit with erythritol
1/3 cup raw cashews, soaked in boiling water for 30 minutes
1/3 cup ground chia seeds plus 2 tablespoons

In a blender, add berries, lemon juice, raspberry powder, milk, and monk fruit. Blend well. Add cashews. Add chia seeds. Refrigerate. Serve with pumpkin seeds and walnuts.

I usually double this recipe.

SWEET POTATO BEAN BURGER

2 medium sweet potatoes (I often use frozen sweet potatoes)
3 tablespoons freshly ground flax seeds
3 tablespoons water
Zest and juice of 1 lime
1 teaspoon ground cumin
1 teaspoon paprika
1 teaspoon chili powder
1 small red onion, chopped finely
2 cloves garlic, chopped
¾ cup oats
1 cup canned black beans or kidney beans, rinsed and drained well
Salt and pepper
Oat flour for dusting

Bake the sweet potatoes ahead of time and remove from jackets. Mash. Mix flaxseeds with the water and set aside 4-5 minutes.

Place lime zest and lime juice, cumin, paprika, chili powder, onion, garlic, ground seeds and oats in food processor. Pulse until ingredients come together. Add black beans or kidney beans. Pulse once or twice to incorporate. I like the texture of the beans to still be somewhat intact. Add salt to taste.

Transfer the mixture to a mixing bowl and shape 9 patties. Use wet hands to do this. Dust the patties with oat flour. Place in freezer 10-15 minutes. Preheat the oven to 400 degrees. Line a baking sheet with parchment paper. Place frozen burgers on pan. Bake 20 minutes, gently flip, bake 20 minutes. Broil 2-3 minutes. Really good with Cashew Queso on top. These freeze well.

CAULIFLOWER FROZEN COOKIE DOUGH BITES

These are amazing treats. Limit yourself to not more than two a day. You will find they are so good you will want more, but don't! When they come out of the freezer, they are very hard. However, they soften in just a minute or two.

2 tablespoons ground flax seed mixed with 1/4 cup water
2 cups cauliflower
1/3 cup monk fruit with erythritol
3/4 cup peanut butter
1 teaspoon vanilla
14 cup almond milk
1 1/2 cup almond flour
1/2 cup oat flour
1/4 cup cacao chips or cacao nibs. (I also purchase 100% cacao chocolate bars and run them through the Vitamix to have chips ready for use.)

Soak the flax seed in water and set aside. Throw 2 cups cauliflower in the blender and process it until the pieces are very small. Combine cauliflower with remaining ingredients. Add in flax seed. Scoop 1 heaped tablespoon onto a parchment lined baking sheet. Repeat. Freeze

VEGETABLE PATTIES

1/3 cup cooked quinoa
3 cloves chopped garlic
1 zucchini, finely ground
1 carrot, finely ground
2 tablespoons whole flax seed
3 tablespoons water
½ cup grated Nutritional Yeast
½ teaspoon salt
¼ teaspoon pepper
1 tablespoon turmeric
¾ cup almond flour

Stir whole flax seed and water together. Set aside for 10 minutes.

Prepare quinoa following package instructions. Drain excess liquid. Allow to cool thoroughly. I spread it on a platter to facilitate the drying. Grate zucchini and carrot to produce about 1 cup, or run through the Vitamix. Squeeze the vegetables to remove excess moisture.

In a separate bowl, combine flax seed/water mixture, garlic, vegetables, nutritional yeast, turmeric, salt, and pepper. Stir in quinoa and almond flour. Let stand to thicken.

Preheat oven to 426 degrees. Form into patties using an ice cream scoop. Flatten. Bake 12 minutes or until golden brown.

BANANA MUFFINS

1/3 cup melted coconut oil
½ cup monk fruit with erythritol
2 tablespoons flax seed
3 tablespoons water
1 cup packed mashed ripe bananas (about 3 bananas)
¼ cup almond milk
1 teaspoon baking soda
1 teaspoon vanilla extract
½ teaspoon salt
½ teaspoon cinnamon
1 ¾ cups whole wheat flour
1/3 cup old fashioned oats
3 tablespoons ground flax seeds

Soak flax seeds in water and set aside for 10 minutes.

Preheat the oven to 325 degrees. Add cupcake liners to your cupcake pan. In a large bowl, beat the coconut oil and monk fruit together with a whisk. Add the ground flax seeds and beat well. Mix in the mashed bananas and milk, followed by the baking soda, vanilla extract, ground seeds, and salt and cinnamon. Add the flax seeds soaked in water.

Add the flour and oats to the bowl and mix with a large spoon, just until combined. Divide the batter evenly between the muffin cups, filling each cup about two-thirds full. Sprinkle the tops of the muffins with a small amount of oats (about 1 tablespoon in total), followed by a light sprinkling of monk fruit. Bake muffins for 22 to 25 minutes, or until a toothpick inserted into a muffin comes out clean.

SWEET POTATO BROWNIES

¾ cup mashed cooked sweet potatoes
½ cup peanut butter
½ cup 100% cacao powder
1 cup monk fruit with erythritol
1/3 cup whole wheat flour
1 teaspoon baking powder
1 teaspoon vanilla extract
¼ teaspoon salt
½ cup 100% cacao chips, chopped

Preheat the oven to 350 degrees and line a 9-inch square pan with parchment paper.

In a large bowl, mix all ingredients until thoroughly blended. Transfer the batter to the prepared pan, and use a spatula to smooth the top.

Bake at 350 degrees until the edges look dry and the center of the brownies have puffed up. About 35-40 minutes. Let them cool before slicing into 16 squares. Store in airtight container in the refrigerator.

Hold onto your hat when you taste these. They are AMAZING!

CHAPTER 5
Lifestyle Changes – Sleep

Sleep is a wonderful thing. Lack of sleep ain't so good. (I love the word "ain't.") My Momma loved to sleep. It was always something she enjoyed, and dementia did not change that. I truly think she could have slept half her day away and thought it to be totally normal.

Sleep needs to be part of your daily routine, and not just some sleep. You need healthy sleep. What happens when we don't sleep well? What changes can we make to improve our sleep?

"When you lie down, you will not be afraid, when you lie down, your sleep will be sweet." (Proverbs 3:24, NIV)

"I lie down and sleep; I wake again, because The LORD sustains me. (Psalms 3:5, NIV)

As Alzheimer's progresses, we see changes in sleep patterns. This is especially true when individuals start "sundowning." Sundowning happens somewhere in the early afternoon and causes the symptoms of dementia to amplify. As the sun sets, we often see agitation, wandering, confusion, and these changes become more prominent. Sleep becomes even more important if sundowning is part of the picture. For you, the caregiver, sleep is also very important in preventing dementia.

When you sleep, your brain goes through a process of cleaning. The vacuum cleaner comes out and removes toxins that have built up. Because your brain is so active during the day, there is no time for cleaning. When your brain is less active while you sleep, there is time for a good thorough house cleaning to take place. If you are sleeping well, this cleaning happens every night. If you are not sleeping well, the vacuum stays in the closet. You want your vacuum to operate every night of your life. That's why healthy sleep is so important.

We need at least 6-8 hours of deep sleep each night. Sleep comes in cycles throughout the night. You do not stay in the deep dream state of sleep for extended lengths of time. It comes and goes, but that is normal. The optimal sleep occurs when we go to bed at the same time each day and sleep until our body wakes us. Now that sounds like you can sleep all day, like my Momma tended to do. However, when the body is receiving good quality sleep each and every day, the body will desire sleep about the same time each night and awaken about the same time each day. No alarm clock needed.

Making the bedroom conducive to good sleep is important. If your loved one is fond of afternoon naps, consider napping in a recliner or on the sofa. Don't nap in the bedroom. However, naps can affect the quality and quantity of sleep at night. Let's earmark the bedroom for nighttime activities ONLY. This room, for individuals with dementia, is just for sleeping and changing of clothes. The room is not cluttered (clutter is just an accident waiting to happen), it is a good temperature, it has a soft cozy bed and pillow and blankets, and there might be a white noise machine in the room. A white noise machine helps sleep to occur more readily, as it blocks out other noises that distract us from sleep.

It is believed a cool room helps us sleep better, and I totally believe this to be true. However, your loved one with dementia may be cold most of the time. If they are cold in bed, they will not be comfortable. The process of knowing how many blankets are needed, the perfect weight pajamas, and what temperature the room should be can become a time consuming event. However, their sleep will not be as restorative if they are not comfortable. The same is true for you, also. Don't forget socks. If the feet are cold, the entire body is less relaxed.

In his book THE POWER OF WHEN, Dr. Michael Breus gives a great deal of information on how to induce and maintain quality sleep. Here are some tips that have helped me sleep much better, and they just might be helpful for you, also. Don't take my word for it, though, purchase his book! (I have paraphrased this list from Dr. Breus' book.)[6]

1. Take a warm bath before bedtime. A warm bath turns on melatonin, and melatonin helps you sleep. I take this bath in a dark bathroom.

2. Speaking of a dark bathroom, begin dimming the lights throughout the house about 90 – 120 minutes before bedtime. BE CAREFUL OF DOING THIS IF YOUR LOVED ONE WITH DEMENTIA WILL BE MOVING AROUND WITHOUT ASSISTANCE. WE DON'T WANT FALLS. Dimming the lights helps the brain to begin the process of "powering down" for the evening.

3. Avoid television, or any screens, 60 minutes before bedtime. If you prefer to read from an iPad or electronic reader, do so while wearing blue lens glasses or sunglasses.

4. Cut liquids for the day two hours before bedtime. This has made a huge difference in the number of times I get up each night to visit the bathroom. It has also been the hardest change for me. I love to drink water or herbal tea all day, and not having any for two hours be-

fore bedtime has been difficult. However, I am sleeping better and getting up only once each night (as opposed to four or five times, previously).

5. Take melatonin (if your doctor approves) 90 minutes before bedtime. If taken at bedtime, it has not yet begun its magic. If taken 90 minutes before bedtime, it has started doing its work, and the brain begins to relax.

6. Investigate if prescription drugs are interfering with melatonin. This was a surprise to me. I take one drug each day, and I take it at night with the melatonin. I discovered this drug decreased the efficacy of melatonin. The drug has been moved to my morning routine, and sleep has improved. Easy!

7. Wear an eye mask in bed. This is an enjoyable part of my evening. I like having the light blocked from my eyes, and the mask is comfortable. Sometime during the night, I seem to take it off. It is always on the floor when I awake.

8. Dr. Breus, in his book THE POWER OF WHEN, recommends Banana Tea. I tried this tea, and I was surprised how well it works. It is so easy to make, and it tastes like... bananas!

Thoroughly wash the banana. With the peel still on, cut the ends off. Cut the banana in half and boil in 3 cups of water for 4 minutes. Let it cool. Drink the water and freeze the peeled banana for muffins or smoothies. Don't add sweetener to the water. It is plenty sweet without it.

9. I was a little surprised to learn an alcoholic drink before bedtime is NOT recommended to

help with a good night's rest. Skip the alcohol, drink the banana tea.

10. Check with your doctor about adding magnesium to your nighttime regimen. DON'T TAKE MY WORD FOR THIS. CHECK WITH YOUR DOCTOR. That being said, my functional medicine physician recommended adding three 120-milligram magnesium glycinate each night. When purchasing magnesium, make sure it is magnesium GLYCINATE. There are various forms of magnesium, and magnesium glycinate is the type that helps with sleep. The brand recommended for me is Pure Encapsulations.

11. In his book MEMORY RESCUE, Dr. Daniel Amen[7] lists several nutraceuticals that help with sleep. Be sure to check with your doctor before adding these supplements.

Melatonin:	0.3 - 6 mg a day
5-HTTP:	50-200 mg a day
Magnesium:	50-400 mg a day
Zinc:	20-40 mg a day
GABA:	250-1,000 mg a day
Lemon Balm:	300-600 mg a day
Vitamin D3:	3,500 IU a day

CHAPTER 6

Lifestyle Changes – Exercise and Socialization

My Momma was never quite good at regular exercise. There was a time in her life, in the early stages of her dementia, she decided to join the local gym with me. I told her there was an easy aerobics class after work, and I invited her to join me. She did. That sounds great, except Momma showed up to class wearing dress pants, a turtleneck sweater, and high-heeled boots. I asked if she brought clothes to change into, and she had not. She was sure she could participate in the clothing she had on. And...she did! Go figure!

> "Do you not know that your bodies are temples of the
> Holy Spirit, who is in you, whom you have received
> from God? You are not your own."
> (I Corinthians 6:19, NIV)

I've spent my life trying to stay on a regular exercise regime. I have not been successful. As of late, that exercise regime has been hampered by my recovery from a car accident. I have, however, learned I feel better when I exercise.

Exercise does NOT have to be at a gym. It does NOT have to be with a trainer. It does NOT require equipment. It does NOT require pain. It DOES require a little determination and finding out what you enjoy doing. Doing that exercise on a regular schedule is important.

Maybe you like to walk. Then walk. Don't worry that you are

not walking far enough or fast enough, just get yourself outside and walk! The more you do this, the further and faster you will walk. Maybe there is a second activity you enjoy. Throw that in your week to mix things up, and VOILA, you have an exercise routine.

Your loved one with dementia needs exercise, also. Maybe you take them for a short stroll while you push an empty wheelchair. When they have walked far enough, they get in the wheelchair. You push them back home, and you've just added strength training to your walk!

Consider bean bags for exercise activities with your special person. For Momma, I made bean bags from soft fleece material and filled with dried beans. I used the bean bags like dumb bells. We would lift them above our head, out to the left and right, and up and down. I would also place one on the top of her foot and challenge her to move that bean bag to the other foot without using her hands. Momma and I did this together. If your loved one is "seeing AND hearing" directions rather than just "hearing" them, they are more likely to respond favorably.

While doing exercise with your loved one, consider adding some background music. It might encourage their attendance. If they stop and sing in the process, sing with them! It is all good.

One beautiful thing about exercising together is socialization. If you have a friend who will walk or swim or do aerobics with you, you are more likely to be consistent. This is a good thing. The socialization that comes when two friends are together is so good for the healing of the body, the brain, and the emotions. The knowledge that someone enjoys being with you is uplifting and healing. It helps fight depression and lowers anxiety. The same is true for your loved one.

Maybe there is a neighbor who will come once a week just to walk with your person, or maybe they will use the bean bags with them. Whatever the activity is, whether it is exercise or just having a good talk, your loved one will benefit from that experience. In fact, if you are around your folks most of the time, having someone else visit with them is beneficial for both them and you. They like you, but they might get tired of you!! Give them another pretty face to enjoy being with.

I have the pleasure of offering Creative Music Experiences with individuals who have dementia. They are so much fun. We meet one-on-one or in small groups. Recently, my client, Mrs. Barbara, made my day. Mrs. Barbara is not a country music fan, but I decided to introduce to her the song, "I Don't Need Your Rockin' Chair." I instructed her to yell those words each time I pointed at her. And SHE DID IT! Then she laughed, I laughed, and we were both better for the experience. At our next visit, there was a group of three ladies who joined the fun. They all said, "I don't need your rockin' chair" when I pointed at them, and the fun and joy was shared.

Spending time with folks we like being around is so good for our mind, our body, our soul, our emotions... and everything about the human body benefits from good socialization.

CHAPTER 7

Lifestyle Changes – Worship

I come to you as a Christian. I have spent my life worshipping my Savior, Jesus Christ. I realize, however, that is not the case for all my readers. I have respect for who you are. Regarding "worship," we know that regular worship with other believers is one of the things that extends life.

> "Worship the Lord your God, and his blessing will be on your food and water. I will take away sickness from among you."
> (Exodus 23:25, NIV)

As life gets busy, we sometimes make gathering for regular worship a lesser priority than other things. If the football game or race comes on during the 11:00 worship hour, we just might opt not to attend. What we know from The Blue Zones Project is regular gathering for corporate worship is very beneficial for the human body and brain.

Being with folks of "like mind" is a soothing, calming, and healing experience. This is true for your loved one with dementia. Make worship opportunities available for them. However, that might take some extra work.

As your loved one with dementia progresses through their disease, they might find gathering in a big sanctuary or temple to be overwhelming. This certainly happened with my Momma. She began having panic attacks when service started. There was too much noise, too many people, too much activity, and she just could not take it. I began conducting worship for folks with dementia shortly after her attacks. These services were short, the songs were from their past, and the noise levels were kept to a minimum. It was a great success for my friends with dementia, and I was thrilled to be a part of their worship experience.

Maybe you can't hold a worship gathering for folks with dementia, but you can hold a time of devotion and music in your living room. Gather the family. Play songs of worship from YouTube, read a devotion, pray, and tell stories of faith. Be sure to include your loved one in the opportunity to pray aloud, sing, and recite scripture. While they might not be able to remember who you are or where they are, their right temporal lobe is more intact than any other part of their brain. The right temporal lobe holds prayer, poetry, art, and acts of worship. Bringing to their lives opportunities to use that part of their brain makes their day more meaningful. It allows them to participate in life more fully.

I have the wonderful opportunity to pray with my clients who have dementia. One particular lady noticed the cast on my right hand. Thumb surgery required the wearing of this cast. She did not ask me about it. There was no conversation about my health. However, at the end of our time of visiting and enjoying music together, I asked if she would pray for me. I regularly prayed for HER, but I asked if she would pray for ME. She began praying the most beautiful prayer, and she asked for healing of my hand. I have to admit, I was surprised she had noticed my cast and was able to recall it during her time of prayer.

That experience reminded me how God works in amazing ways through prayer. Make sure to include your loved one in prayer opportunities every chance you get. They are able to ask the blessing over the food, say the night time prayer, or just pray when asked. They can most likely recite "The Lord's Prayer" or say "The Rosary," but they need to be included and asked to participate.

One last thought. When interacting with your loved one with dementia, use your handy-dandy phone and make a video of the experience. I have many videos of Momma singing, praying, acting silly, and one telling me her name was VERA JEAN SCHRINDBERGER. (Her name was Vera Jean Holder.) This is the conversation: (WARNING – Momma uses a dirty word, but it is too funny not to include.)

ME: Momma, you just asked me if my name is Carol Lynn...

MOMMA: No, you don't get to ask me what I would have asked you.

ME: I don't?

MOMMA: Well I don't give a you know what you asked me.

ME: Alright, you asked me if my name is Carol Lynn ???

MOMMA: Fritenburger

ME: Fritenburger! Who, or what, is a Fritenburger?

MOMMA: Well, do you know any of these names that we just named as Fritenburgers?

ME: No. Did you know Fritenburgers?

MOMMA: No.

ME: Did you just make that up?

MOMMA: Sho did!

ME: Sho, did! My name is not Carol Lynn Fritenburger. Is your name Vera Jean Fritenburger?

MOMMA: No. I'm not a Fritenbruger.

ME: You're not a Fritenburger?

MOMMA: NO.

ME: Alright, who is ya?

MOMMA: SCHRINDBERGER.

ME: Vera Jean Schrindberger. How do you spell that?

MOMMA: S C H R I N D B E (pause) G E R.

ME: Pretty good!

MOMMA: Britchingburger - B E R H.. Shit, if I know how?

And then she cracked up with the biggest smile and laugh possible.

Now don't be offended by her saying the "s" word. As Alzheimer's does its dirty work in the brain, inhibitions are lost, and so are words. Often times the words most commonly remembered are the words our parents told us never to say. They are stored in the part of the brain that is still intact, and those words can be recalled. Likewise, prayer, poetry, art, music and dance are stored in the same part of the brain. Offer opportunities to engage your loved one in these things and help them to engage their brain.

CHAPTER 8

Lifestyle Changes –
Think About What You Think About

"Think about what you think about" is a phrase I picked up from Rev. Max Lucado. I read his books and regularly listen to his worship services online. He told the story about his grandson, "Little Max," who had filled his pockets with rocks while outside having a great time on the property.

As the day progressed, Little Max had so many rocks in his shirt pockets and pants pockets, that he was brought to the ground, and his pants were falling off. His sister came running to the home yelling, "911! 911! Little Max is down!" While this was a frightening set of words to hear, the family was happy to see Little Max really had no emergency; he just needed to remove the rocks from his pockets.

How many rocks are in your pockets? What are you carrying around that is weighing you down? How much better would you feel, how much longer would you live, how much more productive would you be if you let go of those rocks?

"Anxiety weighs down the heart, but a kind word cheers it up."
(Proverbs 12:25, NIV)

If you are living in a state of constant stress and anxiety, the part of your brain called the amygdala is constantly ON. The amygdala is the part of your brain where "fight or flight" happens. If you are being chased by a bear, the amygdala comes on in full force to give you unusual ability to run. This is a wonderful thing. If, however, the amygdala stays on 24/7, this is not a good thing. Anxiety will cause the amygdala to activate even when we don't need it to, and this can cause stressors in our body that are unhealthy. Stress is a killer. It leads to a host of diseases and imbalances in the human body. Stress and anxiety make dementia worse. This is true when the stress and anxiety are coming from the person with dementia or from the person/persons who are caring for them.

So, what do we do? First, I recommend prayer. Take your concerns to God. Tell Him everything that is on your mind and heart. Let it go.

Secondly, talk to a qualified person about your anxiety. I do this regularly with a psychologist, and it has helped me in ways I could never have imagined.

Thirdly, make a list of what you are thankful for. Maybe you physically write this list, or maybe you take time with a family member to say things out loud. Recognizing your blessings is a huge way to begin to heal.

Lastly, recognize how often we worry over things that never happen. We are afraid we will be sick, lose a job, have a financial crisis, experience the death of a loved one, be in a car accident, and on and on the list can go. What we don't realize is this – most of the things we stress over never happen.

This became very real to me recently when my kids did not arrive for Sunday church worship. My husband and I waited in the car as long as we could, but they did not show. We looked with anticipation towards the sanctuary doors hoping to see them. No show. I texted my daughter. No response. I texted again. No response. I was just moments away from going to the narthex and calling to check on her when a text came in saying, "Momma, I told you we were sleeping in today since we just got in from a flight across the globe."

I had not noticed that text, and I was sure they were dead on the interstate! I was stressed over something that did not require me to be stressed. At that point, my amygdala was on full blast, and I could have outrun every Christian in that church! I was checking on my kids, and nothing was stopping me. Too much stress is not good.

Include your loved one in these healing practices. I especially recommend prayer and offering of thanksgivings as regular practices for those with dementia. Being thankful has a way of "removing those rocks" that are holding us down.

Is it time to empty your pockets?

CHAPTER 9

Inflammation Causes Alzheimer's

When I wrote LET'S TALK DEMENTIA several years ago, I stated there was nothing we could do to prevent Alzheimer's. We also believed there was nothing we could do to slow the progression of Alzheimer's. Now we know that is not true, as you have learned thus far in this book. One of the biggest things we can do to reduce our chances of getting Alzheimer's is to lower inflammation throughout the body.

"Dear friend, I pray that you may enjoy good health and that all may go well with you, even as your soul is getting well."

(3 John 1:2, NIV)

Inflammation is a direct cause of Alzheimer's. Leaky Gut Syndrome, diabetes, high blood pressure, and many other things lead to inflammation. Inflammation is not all bad. If you cut your arm, the body sends blood cells to the injured area and inflammation occurs. This is good. What we don't want is to live in a constant state of inflammation. This is NOT good.

How do we know if we have too much inflammation? How do we reduce inflammation?

To measure inflammation, the blood test "hs C-REACTIVE PROTEIN" is recommended. (HS stands for high -sensitivity). This simple blood test will give you an inflammation marker. Depending upon the lab and the doctor, this number should be less than 3.0. However, my doctor recommends less than 1.0. This number gives you an index to determine cardiovascular risk, also.

How do we reduce inflammation? Glad you asked. One of the best ways is to make changes in your diet. Then exercise. Then meditate/attend your house of worship. Don't forget how important it is to spend time with friends. In addition, consider adding Omega 3s to your diet, but check with your doctor first!

My husband and I regularly took a rather expensive omega three capsule in an effort to lower the inflammation in our bodies. After attending a seminar hosted by John Robbins as he interviewed Doctors Dean and Ayesha Sherzai, I was excited to learn I could consume omega three through my food. It is easily accomplished by adding freshly ground flax seed to many of your recipes. I have shared many recipes with you, and you will note MANY of them have freshly ground flax seeds listed as an ingredient. Don't be shy. Add them to most of the recipes you currently have at home.

Chia and flax seeds are an amazing addition to your diet. These seeds are best used after grinding them. As I mentioned earlier, you can purchase them already ground, However, they are not as good for you. So, grind them as needed. Add them to everything. I put them in plant-based baked goods, smoothies, soups, on top of my pizza, and a ton of other places.

The brain needs omega 3s for good brain health and good heart health. Omega 3s provide DHA and EPA, and these seeds are a great source for getting the needed omega 3s.

Here is yet another recipe that will boost your omega 3 intake. However, if you are adding ¼ cup flax seed to your morning smoothie, you are starting you day with all the omega 3 you need.

MEXICAN LAYERED DIP

1 can refried beans

1 can black beans, drained

1 can whole kernel corn, drained

3 tablespoons ground flax seed

3 tablespoons water

1 tomato, chopped small

Lettuce, finely chopped

Cashew cheese (See recipe previously listed)

Mix ground flax seed with water and set aside about five minutes. Mix seeds with refried beans. Layer the ingredients in a pretty glass bowl. Chill thoroughly. Serve with fresh vegetables or on a tortilla.

CHAPTER 10
Assisted Living/Memory Care
What To Expect

It was a normal Sunday afternoon when my Momma said, "Let's check out the open house at the new assisted living across the street." So, we did. I was not thinking about Momma moving. I was just being nosey. This new assisted living was literally across the street. We would walk over, take a tour, have free snacks, and come home. Done. That is not what happened.

The day ended in a way I never expected. For one thing, I won the $100 grocery store gift card drawing. That was great news! The big news was Momma's comment while standing in the kitchen of one of the apartments. "Carol, I want to live here. You figure out how to pay for it." I was stunned. I was speechless. I was sad. I was excited. I was scared. I was... you name it.

> "I lift you my eyes to the mountains – where does my help come from? My help comes from the Lord, the Maker of heaven and earth."
>
> (Psalm 121:1-2, NIV)

Making the decision to move to an assisted living or a memory care is HUGE! It comes wrought with emotions that are never expected, but these emotions have to be dealt with. It comes with lots of questions, and these answers must be obtained.

Here is the catcher – the answers are not readily available. That's why I do the work I do.

Part of my joy is helping families navigate the decision- making process of assisted living. This chapter will help you, but you can always request a free phone consultation through my website – www.letstalkdementia.org.

Here are a few things for you to consider.

1. <u>Find an assisted living near your home if possible.</u> In a perfect world you will want to visit your loved one several times a week, if not daily. If this requires driving long distances, the visits become quite a challenge and an expense of both money and time.

2. <u>Tour the assisted living.</u> Touring an assisted living should be done after making an appointment. I HIGHLY RECOMMEND YOU CONTACT ME FIRST – carol@letstalkdementia.org. I will help you determine what communities are best for you. If you contact the community directly, you will not have the support you need. After touring the community through a set appointment, show up unexpectedly. Maybe show up for an activity or hang out in the lobby. The staff will most likely not want you walking through the building without an employee, but you can sit in the lobby and observe.

When touring or visiting, observe how staff interacts with residents. Do they recognize them by name? Are they calling them "sweetie" or "cutie"? This means they do not know their name. Being called by their name is very important.

Do residents seem bored? Are they engaged and participating in life?

Is the community clean? Do you see dust or surfaces that

need cleaning?

Have you been introduced to the director of the community, the director of housekeeping, the director of maintenance, the director of activities? Have these folks taken time to talk with you about their duties? Do they show enthusiasm for their job?

Ask for a meeting with the director of nursing. This person will play a huge role in the care your loved one will receive. Show them a list of medications you person takes and explain any diagnosis they may have received. Be prepared to ask as many questions as you can possibly think of, and don't leave until you have received the answers. Never let anyone push you aside as if your questions and concerns are not valid. THEY ARE VALID!

When walking through the community, did you observe any activities? If yes, were they well attended and directed by a staff member who seemed to be enjoying their work? If you did not see an activity, check the activity calendar and see if one was scheduled but not happening. If this is the case, ask why?

Don't make a quick decision. There are usually a few communities to tour, and you need to compare and contrast the communities in order to make the best decision.

3. After the tour, ask to speak about pricing. This is very important. When you and I work together, I will already have gathered this information for you, but I still recommend you ask the same questions again.

Here is a hint – when moving to an assisted living or memory care, plan to move in the last ten days of the month. Most communities are corporately owned, and the staff is expected to meet a census percentage for the month. If their census is high the first of the month, they will be less likely to offer discounts or incentives to get you to commit to their community. Likewise, if their census is down a bit, they will offer discounts. ALWAYS ASK FOR DISCOUNTS.

Most every community will have a one-time "community fee." This fee is used to help pay to refurbish a room once a resident moves out. This might include paint, carpet, cleaning, etc. However, this is the easiest fee to get a discount on. These fees might run from $200 to $5000. Although it is a one-time fee, if we can discount it, that is great. Ask for the discount.

In addition, most communities will run some sort of special in room rates during the last few days of the month. Once the rate is given for the apartment you have chosen, ask for a discount. It is interesting how many times additional discounts are given.

4. Understanding what is included in assisted living is important. The basic rent rate should (not always) include power, three meals a day, snacks, maid service, laundry, handyman service, driver service, and activities. The basic rate does not include physical care of the body unless you are at an all-inclusive community.

Charges for care vary depending upon the resident and their particular needs. Some communities charge care by levels. Level 1 costs a certain price and includes a certain number of care activities. Level 2 will cost more and include even more care activities.

Other communities charge per care need. Sort of like an a la carte menu. You only pay for what you need. This can be very beneficial if you only need help with a few items. For instance, if you need help with medication management, but you can take care of everything else, you might not want to pay for an entire Level 1 care cost. This is something to look at when choosing a community. However, be aware that care needs change. As dementia progresses, you can expect the care needs to increase.

In an all-inclusive community, you pay one fee and it includes everything I have mentioned thus far AND any care your person might need. For example, if they did not need help bathing when they moved in, but later that becomes a need, the monthly cost does not go up. It would go up with a la carte pricing, and it might go up with care that is divided into levels, but it does not go up at an all-inclusive community. If you are looking at a memory care community, and they offer all-inclusive, I always think that is the best option.

However, all-inclusive does not mean your person will never have to move. If their care needs go beyond the scope of services offered at that assisted living or memory care, as dictated by state law, they may need to move to a skilled nursing community.

5. Once you have made the decision to move, be careful how many items you move to the new apartment. You absolutely want the new apartment to feel like home. Take their favorite chair, bedspread, pillow, pictures on the wall. Make it feel like home as much as possible. Do not, however, take throw rugs and a ton of knick-knacks to place on tables. Make sure the traffic pattern is easily accessible.

Many of my clients think, "Momma will need a microwave. She loves to heat her coffee." I always smile and recommend the staff will make sure she has hot coffee anytime she might want it. Invariably, the microwave is purchased, and then it is never used.

Remember, your loved one will spend less time in their apartment than you might imagine. The goal of a good community is to get their residents out of their apartment and participating in life. They invite them to attend activities, go for bus rides, shop with the other residents, etc. Their life will be enriched by their participation in these activities.

That being said, many folks move to assisted living, and the family sets up a television for them. This often means paying for cable or streaming services. (Not to mention remote controls they might not be able to operate.) Depending upon the progression of their disease, this television is never watched. I did this for Momma when she moved to memory care. I was absolutely sure she would want her television. She did not watch it, and I had committed to a contract with the cable provider! UGH! I recommend not putting a television immediately. See how involved they become in activities. They might not need one. And, if they don't have a television, it might cause them to be more social rather than sitting alone in their room.

6. Expect staff to perform the care activities agreed upon in the "move-in assessment." This assessment is usually performed by a nurse or upper management employee. The employee learns about the medical needs of the individual, the medications they are taking, the treatments they might need, their daily habits, and their likes and dislikes in regards to bathing, dressing, bedtime, etc. These care needs are documented on their MAR – Medical Assessment Record – and they are to be performed by staff.

7. Expect medications to be given timely. In most

states, there is a window of time available for medication distribution. It is usually two hours before or two hours after the prescribed time. Remember, the person delivering the medication has many persons who probably need medications at the exact same time. Allowing this window of time is helpful.

8. Expect activities to take place as listed on the activities calendar. When state officials visit a community for their rating, they will look at that activity calendar and discern if activities are happening. You should do the same thing. However, it is great for you to volunteer to help the activities director. Maybe you can lead a singing group, craft group, story-telling group, Bible-reading group, or whatever group you have a particular talent for. This will also give you an opportunity to interact with other residents and see how your loved one interacts with them as well. (My Momma, oh my goodness, decided she did not want to attend the hand-bell sessions I had worked so hard on. She said, "that ain't no fun." WHAT? I could not believe my own Momma was turning me down! Honestly, she was not good at playing handbells, either.)

9. Expect the apartment to be kept clean. It should have been spotless before moving in. If not, stop and ask for the needed cleaning to happen. Most caregivers are happy to make sure cleaning is kept up to date. Just keep an eye on things.

10. Expect the community to supply only those items they agreed upon. For instance, most communities will supply toilet tissue, but they do not supply Kleenex. They also do not normally supply shower items or soap. These are personal items. Find out ahead of time what is supplied, and be prepared to

bring the other items with you. Sometimes it is easier to order these things and have them delivered.

11. Expect to hear "I want to go home." "Get me out of this place." "Why am I here?" Especially in the face of dementia, our loved ones spend a great deal of time thinking about themselves. It becomes a ME, ME, ME world. If one thing has gone wrong, their mind is stuck on that one thing (but you do the same thing). It is your job to acknowledge their question, and maybe say, "When you leave, where are you going? What will you do when you get there?" Then agree it is a great idea and you will work on it. Then say, "In the meantime, though, let's go to the dining room where they have a group of singers performing. I'll attend with you." Now you have taken their mind from the ME, ME, ME problem of the moment, and moved their thought to spending time with you.

Know this – the place they want to go is probably NOT the place you have pictured. Most often they are thinking of going to the home they grew up in. They want to go back to their parents. You couldn't do this for them if you wanted to, so don't beat yourself up. They are seldom yearning to go back home with you. I know that may be difficult to hear, but it can be a source of relief if you realize it is not something you can change or fix.

CHAPTER 11

Assisted Living/Memory Care - What Not To Expect

Don't expect staff to do everything. They can't. Your expectations might be reasonable, but they might not be in the scope of their job. Caregivers are truly overworked, but they are trying so hard. I have seen a few caregivers who made me cringe, but most caregivers have a huge heart and want what is best. Be kind. Ask courteously. If you do not get the result you want, take that request to the Executive Director.

> "The LORD has given me a well-instructed tongue, to know the word that sustains the weary. He wakens me morning by morning, wakens my ear to listen like one being instructed."
> (Isaiah 50:4, NIV)

Be patient. If an activity did not happen, there is probably a good reason. If the laundry is a day late, and the basket is overflowing, could it be the machine is broken? Ask the "why" of a situation before making a big deal.

I will admit, with a sigh, I was not always that patient. If I entered Momma's room and things were not just perfect, I would be in someone's face. This did not accomplish much. It did, however, make me anxious. It made Momma anxious, and it irritated the caregiver. It might even have affected how they felt about my sweet Momma. It took me a minute to realize my approach with caregivers had an effect on their approach with my

Momma.

The other thing I learned is it never hurts to be appreciative. Kind words make a difference. "Momma's hair has never looked better. You did a great job." Or a plate of snacks delivered to the care team will help foster a better environment for your loved one, you, and everyone else in the community.

Think a moment about your job. How many times were your recognized for doing a great job? How many times were you called on the carpet when you messed up? You may have been excellent 9 out of 10 days, but that one day – that one hard day – you had a flub up. Then the boss was all over you with criticism. You did not need that. Remember those days when you are talking to these caregivers. Patience. Smiling. Kindness. "Do unto others as you would have them do unto you." (Matthews 7:12). Good words to live by.

If there is one thing I can guarantee, something will go amiss. We are human beings taking care of individuals who have diseased brains. The process will never be perfect, and it is not easy. Our response to the various situations is important. However, if you are kind, and yet you see no change, take your concerns to the Executive Director. Have a sit-down, face-to-face meeting with this person. If the problem is in regards to a medical issue, ask for the Director of Nursing, the physician, physician assistant, or nurse practitioner, *and* the executive director of the community to be part of the meeting. If the problem is with cleanliness of the apartment, ask for the Director of Maintenance to be there. If you feel the food is not good, ask for the chef to attend. You get the idea.

Make a list of concerns to give to each person in attendance. Document what is being said while you are in the meeting. You want them to see you making these notes. Read these notes back to them, so they know you have the correct information. You will then be able to hold them accountable for making sure the situation is corrected. This works well!

Lastly, don't expect your loved one to be happy every time you visit. Are you happy every day? Well, they are not either. There are a million and one reasons why they may not be happy. And these same reasons could, and mostly would, exist no matter where they lived.

You would be surprised to know how many times a resident will complain to their family about being unhappy, but as soon as the family member leaves, the resident is up talking, dancing, singing, and having a great time. It is much like the first time you took your child to kindergarten. They cried so hard when you left, but they were coloring and having a great time before you got back in your car. I know – this happened to me with my daughter! I also know this happened to me with my mother. She often participated in activities that surprised me. I would often sneak in and observe her having a great time. She was happy as a clam. ("Happy as a clam" is a saying from Momma. I have no clue how happy a clam is or why a clam would be happy. But, whatever!)

CHAPTER 12

Paying For Assisted Living/Memory Care

You have found the community that will work best for your person. It seems to meet all their needs and your expectations, but the cost. Oh, my goodness! Who knew it was so expensive?

"Honor the Lord with your wealth, with the firstfruits
of all your crops."
(Proverbs 3:9, NIV)

Assisted living base rates can be as low as $2000 a month and as much as $15,000 a month. It depends upon so many factors, but the biggest factor is the part of the country you live in. The second factor is the size of the apartment you choose. Remember, care costs are usually not included in base rates (unless you choose an all-inclusive community), so costs can be even higher.

While it is best to choose a community that is near your home, you may have to choose one a bit further out. If you live in a big city, prices are usually higher than those a few miles outside the city. Those few extra miles might be the difference between affordability and out-of-range costs. Be aware of this.

Immediately, you need to know Medicare does not pay for assisted living. I quite often receive calls saying, "My neighbor's mother lived at an assisted living and Medicare paid for it." Uh, nope, Medicare did not pay for assisted living or memory care. Never has. I feel pretty safe saying they never will. Most often the individual was in a rehabilitation facility that was housed within an assisted living, and Medicare paid for rehab.

Medicare will pay for a certain number of rehab days. Usually this occurs after a hospitalization stay. This is not the same as moving to an assisted living.

Other folks will say, "I want to move Momma to a Medicaid community." It seems so easy. Let Medicaid pay. That is not as easily done as you might think. Medicaid requires a stringent qualification process. Assets are looked at. Income is counted. Residency is required for the state the assisted living is located.

One important thing to know is this: An irrevocable trust can be your best friend. Placing assets inside an irrevocable trust can protect those assets, so Medicaid cannot touch them or use them to disqualify the individual for benefits. However, this varies by state, so seek an elder care attorney to learn what your state laws say.

In my state, and in most states, the assets inside that trust are protected. This allows the family to move their loved one to a Medicaid community and not spend all the assets of their loved one. Be aware though, just because a community accepts Medicaid does not mean they will have a bed open for your loved one. It also does not mean it is a community you will like. Do your research!

If your person has a long-term care policy, that is great news. Let's review that policy to see what benefits are included. If the policy was written many years ago, the words "assisted living" or "memory care" may not be in the policy. These are fairly new terms, and they may not have been used when the policy was written. This will require a call to the company issuing the policy (usually a life insurance company) to discern what the benefits are.

Just because the policy says they will pay, for example, $100 a day for assisted living, does not mean it might not pay more. Many policies include a cost-of-living increase. Again, a call to the company issuing the policy is so important. Get the facts!

If the person needing to move to a care home is a veteran or the spouse of a veteran, they may qualify for Aid and Attendance. The veteran must have served as least one day during a time of war (even if they were never "boots on the ground"), had honorable discharge, and have a physical need for the care directly related to their person. This benefit is often available to the spouse of a veteran. The process for getting this benefit can be extremely overwhelming if you try to do it on your own. It can be equally as overwhelming if you try to do it through the VA. I did this, and I was horrified at the experience.

It is my recommendation you email Veterans and Families of Florida (info@vfflorida.org). Tell them Carol with Let's Talk Dementia sent you, and you want information about Aid and Attendance.

These folks know what must happen in order for this benefit to be received. I have often said, "If they tell you to stand on your head while you sign page three, just do it. They have a reason." Seriously, though, they are amazing folks. And... drum roll, please... there is no charge for their service. They are a non-profit.

If the spouse of the veteran is divorced from the veteran, there is no available benefit. If the veteran passed away, they may still qualify. If both the husband and wife were veterans, that is fantastic. There is money available.

Take into account the value of assets your loved one might have. Look at savings accounts, IRAs, stocks, bonds, homes, etc. Some assets might need to be sold or liquidated to provide funds for their care. Remember, it is their money and should be used for their well-being.

One of the goals for my clients is this: When they get to the other side of this journey, I want them to look back and know they did everything possible to provide the best life and the best care for their loved one. If that means spending every dime their loved one has on getting that care, then do it! It hurts my heart when family members are more concerned about their inheritance than the welfare of the person suffering with dementia. Put their needs first. I say again, it is their money. Not yours!

CHAPTER 13

Encouraging Thoughts

The following are transcripts from a few podcasts that I recorded. I hope they encourage you on your journey. By the way, you can find my podcasts on Spotify, iTunes, and my website – www.letstalkdementia.org. I post new podcasts and videos each month.

> "Therefore encourage one another with these words."
> (1 Thessalonians 4:18, NIV

"RAIN, RAINBOWS, AND DOLLY PARTON"

Today, I'm thinking about Dolly Parton. You know one of the songs she sang was "Working Nine To Five...what a way to make a living." I like that song. And then, "Jolene, Jolene, Jolene, Jolene". That's a great song, also. It is easy to sing with my folks with dementia because they can sing, "Jolene, Jolene, Jolene."

Dolly Parton is known to have said, "The way I see it, if you want the rainbow, you gotta put up with the rain." As I sit here recording this episode, it is raining. I live in southwest Florida, and it is rainy season. It rains every afternoon. You can just about count on it. Then it dries up, goes away, life is dry again, and you can go on with what you need to do.

Rain is necessary. It does take some rain to bring out the rainbows, and the rainbows in life, well, they are pretty happy. When you think about dementia caregiving, the rainbow analogy is true. When you think about life at all, in any kind of situation, you realize you've got to have the tough times to enjoy the good ones. You've got to go down in the valley before the mountain top seems quite so fabulous. If you are always on the mountain top, you might get really used to it and think that's the way life is all the time – everybody's life is like this. But that's not true. Is it?

It is down in the valley where we realize we are human, we need the help of others, and we need to call upon The Lord to take care of us. You can't do this caregiving journey alone. I'm here to say, "you can't." You think you can, but you cannot. It is going to take other people surrounding you and helping you, but, most of all, it is going to take The Lord lifting you up out of that valley, helping you make your way up the side of that mountain, and you WILL reach the top. I don't know when that is going to happen for you, but it will. You might slide back down a little bit. You might have to fight your way back up again, and back down, and back up. That is life.

There are rainbows in life. I know sometimes when you are in the middle of cleaning a dirty butt AGAIN, or trying to get your loved one to do something they don't want to do, or answering the same question for the 5000th time since breakfast, you begin thinking, "This is never going to get better. I am never going to make it through this. This is the worst thing in the world." Well, you know what? It is not the worst thing in the world. It will get better because life will change. We deal with life as it is given to us.

We can't change what we can't change, and I think that's a hard thing to learn. It's like The Serenity Prayer. Accept the things we can change and let go of the things we can't change. I am trying to do this in my own life, and I imagine it is something we all try to learn throughout our entire lives.

In this dementia caregiving journey, it is much easier when you call upon the help of others. What does that help look like? Well, maybe it is someone to come in a couple of times a week and give you a break. Maybe they come in your home at dinner time and try to get your loved one to eat dinner, and you eat alone or with your husband. Then you are not responsible for helping your loved one eat that meal. You get a break.

Maybe it means having a free phone consultation with me. (Email me at carol@letstalkdementia.org to request this time together.) Maybe it is going to church and someone sitting with your mom on a different pew while you get a break. Whatever. You need that time to get away and to recharge your batteries. You are not the Energizer Bunny. You cannot keep going and going. You are one of those batteries that has to be charged – like on your phone. You have to charge that phone regularly, and you need regular "recharging," also.

You have to take care of yourself. We are going to have the rain, but, by golly, we want some rainbows. The rainbows in your life, when you are deep in the throes of dementia caregiving, sometimes have to be calculated. They have to be planned to allow that rainbow to come through. Otherwise, we get right in the middle of the rain, and that little rain turns in to a big 'ole thunderstorm, and the next thing we know, it is a tornado or hurricane because we are so overwhelmed. Don't let that happen. You have to be in control of the weather!

I hope you find folks in your life that will help you through the rain and help you see the rainbow. I am happy to be one of those people. Write me – carol@letstalkdementia.org.

"MARY KNEW A LITTLE SOMETHING ABOUT CAREGIVING"

Maybe we don't get what Mary went through exactly. We don't really get what anybody goes through except ourselves. However, I want you to know that I understand the challenges of caregiving. Your caregiving journey is different from mine. I had three caregiving journeys, and all three were different. And they are different from yours, but there are similarities. There are days when you are down in the midst of the mundane and it feels like nothing like God's work. This isn't productivity. This is repetition, explanation after explanation, cleaning and feeding. It is not fun!" However, through that situation, you are doing God's work.

In fact, I consider the work you are doing divine. You are doing God's work right there in your home. Right there in your community. In the neighbor's home where you offer assistance. Wherever you are, you are doing The Divine. Maybe it is not on the floor of a stable like it was for Mary.

Maybe it is helping bathe someone. Maybe it is helping feed someone who can no longer hold a spoon.

You don't know where you are going to be placed in this world to help other people. Mary, I'm sure was surprised. We know she was! She had never been with a man! I doubt through nine months of pregnancy she ever thought, "I'm going to this wonderful manger, and it is going to be in a dirty stinky barn, and there are going to be animals all around. I'm going to give birth there. I just can't wait. It's going to be wonderful!" That is not likely what Mary had on her mind. It is, however, what she experienced.

What you had on your mind, before your caregiving journey began, was not this caregiving journey you are on. You were not thinking, "A few years from now I would like to be totally responsible for caregiving for someone who has dementia. Someone who will ask me the same questions repeatedly. Some who cannot feed themselves. I have to bath and dress them. I have to keep an eye on them because they might walk out the door! You didn't think "That will just be wonderful." But in the midst of the mundane, for Mary, Jesus Christ entered the world.

This happens in your caregiving journey, also. Remember, God is with YOU. He is right there in the middle of all that mess you got going on. Divinity. He is Divine. He has plans for us that we can't imagine, fathom, or ever put together. It's amazing, when you think about it, and I hope you will.

In the midst of the mundane, what story are you writing?

◆ ◆ ◆

"HAPPINESS QUOTIENT"

Who does not want to be happy? Well, in my world, I've come across a few people who just really were not interested in being happy. Which is something I seriously don't get. Happy feels so much better on your body than being in a bad mood.

I was reading an author recently who had this long quote about happiness quotient with percentages in it. The percentages did not add up to 100, so I was a little confused by it. She did go on to say, according to her, a full 40% of your happiness quotient is determined by your thoughts and actions. Those things are completely within our control. Well! I am all over that! I totally agree with that statement.

The way we think definitely affects what we do. What we do directly affects how we think. We need to be aware of that. In your caregiving journey, it is often very hard to have upbeat and positive thoughts. Especially all the time. That is hard in everyday life, as well. We all deal with junk, don't we? There is stuff going on we wish we could change. There is stuff going on we wish never happened. Yet, here we are in the middle of it. Our response is going to have a big effect on the outcome of that situation.

I had a physician recently tell me those folks who have been injured, for whatever reason – car accident, for example – healed quicker if they felt free to complain about their injuries. Huh. I found that to be very interesting because it was contradictory to what I have always thought. You know positive thinking is so good for us. What we know as the opposite of that is true also. Negative thinking can be harmful.

Being upbeat and positive has a direct impact on our healing, also. Maybe what we can learn is there is a balance between the two. It is OK to complain and let others know "my back hurts." "My head hurts." "My legs hurt." It is equally as important to say "I am thankful for energy for the day. I am thankful I can get up today and go about life. I'm thankful it is raining because we need the rain. I am thankful my loved one, even though they complain about the food, can still eat and swallow. I'm thankful my loved one, who may not communicate sweet loving thoughts to me, can still communicate in some form. I am thankful my loved one, even though they have messed up their underclothes AGAIN today, allows me to help them with that situation and they are kind to me while I clean them."

There is always something in life to be thankful for. We are totally in control of offering thanksgivings in the midst of life situations.

Philippians 4:8 (NIV) says –
    "Finally, brothers and sisters."

Let's stop right there. I like that word "Finally." It's as if the author is trying to say, "Pay attention you dudes. I'm trying to tell you something important. Now back to the scripture.

> "Finally, brothers and sisters, whatever is true, whatever is noble, whatever is right, whatever is pure, whatever is lovely, whatever is admirable, if anything is excellent or praiseworthy, think about such things."

Oh, what if we went back and put negative words in there?

> "Finally, brothers and sisters, whatever is nasty, whatever is ugly, whatever is frustrating, whatever gets on your nerves, whatever you think is just really irritating, that's what I want you to think on."

That way of thinking would not be good for us. Yet, if you are like me, you spend way more time thinking about the people in your world who irritate you and the situations in your world that should not be the way they are, and not enough time finding those things that are pure and lovely and wholesome and good. We all need to center our thoughts on these things.

We just had the election of the President of the United States in 2020, and there were a number of people very happy of the outcome. Their person got elected. There were a number of people who were very unhappy of the outcome. Their person did not get elected. I know who I voted for, and I know who did and did not get into office. I'm not worked up one way or the other. What I know is my thoughts and actions on this are "God is in control." He knows the outcome of that situation, and He knows the outcome of every situation. He knows the outcome of your caregiving situation, your work situation, your home situation, your health situation. He knows your frustrations with caregiving. He knows what they are. He is hoping that in that process you will seek His face and look for the good things. He wants us to focus upon those things that will bring peace and happiness and joy into our life. The true, the noble, the right, the pure, the lovely, the admirable, the excellent, the praiseworthy. Those things are going to land on you in a pleasant way, and you will feel better.

Guess what? When you feel better, you reduce anxiety and stress. You reduce inflammation within your body. When you reduce inflammation in your body, you drastically decrease the chances of getting Alzheimer's.

So, what are we going to do? We are going to take full control of our thoughts and actions. We can do this! Also, it is a good lead up to being thankful!

◆ ◆ ◆

"SPIRITUAL FITNESS"

I talk all the time about eating right and exercising and reducing inflammation. All those things to help prevent Alzheimer's, and all of that is true. You may not like to hear it, but you need to do it. There is a prevention strategy we might not have spent a lot of time talking about. It is called "Spiritual Fitness." I have fallen in love with Dr. Daniel Amen's teachings. Dr. Amen runs the Amen Clinics. There are many locations. I am in Florida, and the closest one is Atlanta, Georgia. If my family gets a diagnosis of cognitive issues, we will be going to the Amen Clinics for evaluation and testing. Their method of handling cognitive disorders/diseases is much different from what you find elsewhere. He is a big proponent of "Spiritual Fitness."

What is spiritual fitness? What does spirituality mean? It is different for different people. If you have read my work, you know my faith is an important part of who I am, who I have been, and who I always will be. I am very happy about that.

Statistically, a growing number of Americans view themselves as spiritual but not religious – according to PEW research. Belief in God remains strong with 87% of Americans responding YES to a 2017 Gallop Poll that asked if they believed in God. Seventy-seven percent of Americans said they pray at least once monthly. Fifty-seven percent of Americans say they pray daily.

Church membership has dropped 50%. Right now, the COVID situation has made it difficult, but online church is available.

What we know is being a part something greater than us produces a sense of contentment, lowers stress, increases feelings of being accepted and belonging, and that is good for us. Stress reduction is always good. It helps prevent, not just Alzheimer's, but many diseases. Let me list a few ways.

1. MEDITATE – It helps you relax. Relaxing helps reduce stress. If you reduce stress that helps reduce inflammation. Meditation helps to reduce negative thinking. Negative thoughts stick with us, even from our childhood. Meditating can help us release those thoughts, and this reduces the negative effects they have on our brain.

2. HELP OTHERS. Why? When you do things for other people, it makes you feel good. I have a hard time getting my husband to get that. I will say, Let's ask the neighbor to help us do that." He will say, "Oh no. we will figure it out." I asked him, if the neighbor asked YOU for help, would you be offending by that. He said, "NO." "So why are you offended to ask for help?" I asked. Putting your faith into action is good for you. It helps you to release grudges you might be holding against other people.

3. FIND A MENTOR. Seek someone in your life who can mentor you. Someone that can help walk you through the journey, much like I try to do with you through my podcasts and books. Just as you need

someone helping you walk the journey of dementia, you need this help in your spiritual life.

4. DON'T FORGET TO PRAY. That is something I have always done. I feel sad for folks for whom prayer is not a part of their life. I know I have folks listening who may not be of the Christian faith. I don't know who you pray to, but in my world, I pray to God. Nonetheless, we know the act of praying to whomever you pray, is stress reducing. It helps to increase memory. Helps to focus. Helps us have a better mood.

5. DISCOVER WHY GOD MADE YOU – Why is it God made you? What is it He wants you to do? I know with absolutely zero doubt, helping folks traveling the journey of dementia is what I am supposed to do. I can tell you when I am recording my shows, or writing books, or on the phone with caregivers, that is when I am at my best. That is when I feel my best. That's when the remainder of my day goes better because I have found my purpose and I am living it.

◆ ◆ ◆

"REJOICE IN THE LORD ALWAYS - SAY WHAT?"

Let's talk about anxiety and being tense and rejoicing ALWAYS. There is a verse in Philippians 4:4 that says "Rejoice in the Lord always, again I will say rejoice." That is so easy to do when you've just won the lottery. It is very easy when it is your birthday, and your friends are showing up with a cake and ice cream (both of which are going to cause inflammation that is not good for you). They have brought presents, and it is easy to rejoice.

It is hard to rejoice if you've just found out someone you love has cancer, or Alzheimer's, or Parkinson's. Or the person you are caregiving for has just pooped their pants, and now you have to clean it. It is hard to rejoice in that.

How in the world could the Apostle Paul have expected us to reduce our anxiety by rejoicing in The Lord always? How can we rejoice in those hard times when we feel like the world is caving in on us? How in the world do we rejoice?

I think we need to look at that verse a bit more closely. He is not saying we need to rejoice in everything or be glad about the bad situations. We don't have to be thankful for cancer or Alzheimer's or dirty bottoms, but the verse says, "Rejoice in the Lord, always." Always! Hmmm. I don't know how I'm going to do that, but that is what the verse says.

Wait, it says, "rejoice IN THE LORD." Not "rejoice in your situation." Paul did not say, "when bad news comes your way, when the worst happens that you could ever think of, rejoice!" He did not say that. He never told us to rejoice in the situation. He said, "Rejoice in THE LORD." Knowing that no matter the situation, no matter what your caregiving journey is, no matter what the diagnosis is, no matter what challenge you are facing, The Lord is still in control. He still has that life situation in His hands, and through it, we can be confident He will provide. He will be there for us.

It is not an emotion we have. This confidence is not "I'm so excited!" Instead, it is a deep-seated knowledge and a confidence that God's got this situation. He never lets us down. He never has, and He never will. We can rejoice in that. Scripture goes on to say, "again I will say rejoice." Paul knew we are a little dense sometimes, and we don't get this through our head like we should. We are not good at remembering God's got us. We are not good at remembering God loves us more than we can imagine, and He loves our loved one with dementia more than we can possibly every duplicate. Paul tells us to "rejoice in the Lord always, again I will say rejoice."

Are you rejoicing today? Well, I get it. It's hard. My family has experienced many stressful events this calendar year. Life went a little "wacky" for us just a few weeks ago. Things are still wacky, but in the midst of all that grief and crying and sadness, in the midst of the unknown, in the midst of the confusion, in the midst of "what do we do now," and in the midst of wondering what is the plan and how to move forward, there was never a time that I thought, "God, you sure left us alone on this one. You said you would always be with us, but you obviously forgot about us this time."

No! No! Not happening! My faith is in God and in God alone. It is not in those life situations. It was not in my caregiving abilities when I was a caregiver. It wasn't! It was in God's abilities to work through me to bring about something good. He does that with you every day. He works through you to bring something good.

I am proud of you who are. I am proud of how hard you work to be a good caregiver. I am proud of what you give up of yourself and your life to be a good caregiver, but I want you to take care of yourself, also. In the process, I want you to rejoice in the Lord, not your situations. That is what we are called to do. When we can take a moment to rejoice in Him and be thankful, the belly feels better, the head is going to hurt less, and the nerves are going to relax. I think we all need that.

"CREATING YOUR REALITY"

Let's talk about "creating your reality." I am not one of those people that believes you can think things into being. You can vow and declare this is going to happen because God loves you and you are a good person. No, God loves you and you probably are a good person, but having good things happen to you simply because you are good person, as a quote I read recently said, "is like expecting the lion not to eat you because you are a vegetarian." Those two things do not go together.

We do create a good bit of our reality, and we do so by the way we live, the choices we make, the things we do, the things we don't do, the things we eat and the things we don't eat, the exercises we do and the time we sit on our rear end doing nothing. The people we interact with, and the people we should not interact with. The influences we allow into our world, the influences we ignore, and the influences we should ignore and we don't. We have a great deal to do with creating our own reality.

I recently listened to an interview between Hailey Thomas, who wrote LIVING LIVELY THROUGH THE POWER OF PLANTS, and Mr. John Robbins, and John Robbins said,

> "You said that life doesn't happen to you. Rather, you happen to life."

You know that got my attention. Hailey Thomas responded with,

> "Well, I strongly believe in, and have come to understand that, we have the incredible power to create our reality, our immediate reality, but also the experiences that

we have with others, and in being or existing in a victim mentality of – oh everything is happening to ME – it makes us very disempowered and feel out of control. I feel we do cocreate the experiences that we have in the collective, and that we fully have autonomy over how we react to and respond to the situations that come into our lives." [8]

It is true! How you react to a situation is important. As you walk into your loved one's apartment or home who might be in the very early stages of dementia, and they still recognize you, they can still go to the bathroom on their own, they are just pleasantly confused and high functioning, your response to that could be, and I understand if it is, "My world is coming to an end. Momma has dementia. We've just found this out. She is going to forget things. She is not able to do things. It is horrible. Today is just the worst."

If I take you to the home of someone whose mother is in the late stage of Alzheimer's type dementia, who does not recognize them, who cannot verbalize their thoughts, who cannot feed themselves, the family would look at your situation as "oh my goodness, you've got it so good! I've got it really bad, but you've got it really good!" It all depends upon how you perceive life, and how you look at that situation.

This is a personal example. I had a stye come on my eye, and it was on the outside of my left eye. A stye can be very uncomfortable, even painful if it gets large enough. I did everything I knew to do, and finally the silly thing went away. About a week later, on the exact same spot but on the inside of my eye, another stye appeared. I thought there must be a connection. That stye grew to about the size of the end of a writing pen where you click the pen to open and close it. It was very big! I had to have a little surgical procedure to remove it. It had actually started to grow through the eyelid to the outside of the eyelid! It was uncomfortable. I had to do drops every hour for three days, and it started healing.

I could have said, "Oh my word. You just don't know how uncomfortable I am. My eye is so scratchy. Now there is a scab. The scab scratches my eye...". All those things were true, and I even had those thoughts, periodically. Then I would stop and think about some of you guys and the caregiving journey you are on. Or some of my friends who are dealing with cancer, and my stye suddenly seemed to be not so bad. Not such a big deal. Of course, it was something I preferred not to deal with, but I refused to have the victim mentality.

Maybe if the situation were more dire, or a really horrible diagnosis, I may not have reacted so well, and I might have needed reminders of what we are talking about today. At the moment, I am trying to have a good outlook on life. I know having a positive outlook can be difficult in your caregiving journey. I've lived it. But here is the thing. Life is hard!

Your victim mentality can cause a negative response in your loved one. Your positive outlook will more than likely bring a positive outlook for your loved one. Which do you want? Which is going to feel better on them. Which is going to feel better on you? You will feed off each other other's emotions. If you have that upbeat "life is so good" mentality, then life WILL be good. It will certainly be better than if you have the negative "life is horrible" mentality.

The Apostle Paul who was imprisoned, beaten repeatedly, and finally killed for his faith, said, "I have learned in all things to therefore be content." Say what? How did he do that? In all things to be content?" Well, it wasn't that he loved being beat. It wasn't that he thought being imprisoned was a great thing. He had learned to be content knowing that God was in control. His outlook on life was going to be such that he refused to have a victim mentality. I'm pretty sure I'll never be as good at it as the Apostle Paul was, but I am working on it. How about you?

CHAPTER 14

Is It Time For Hospice?

The brain sends messages to all the organs in the body to allow us to live and prosper. Without these messages, the body begins to die. Alzheimer's, and many other dementia causing diseases, causes the brain to cease sending those messages. While not remembering a person's name is not fatal, the REASON behind not remembering their name can be fatal. That is why Alzheimer's is a fatal disease.

"Be kind and compassionate to one another."
(Ephesians 4:32, NIV)

When going through the various phases of Alzheimer's, you will observe changes in your loved one. Their ability to participate in the activities of daily living – bathing, eating, ambulating, dressing and toileting – all become more difficult for them. Their language skills become compromised. They may not want to eat or drink. Being aware of these changes, and reporting them to the physician, is very important.

Once the doctor recommends hospice, it is my recommendation you follow through with a consultation with your local hospice organization. Stop for a moment, and breathe. For many folks, hearing the word "hospice" puts them into panic mode. Just because a hospice organization becomes part of a care team does not mean your loved one's death is imminent. It does mean they have progressed in their disease, and they are in need of more help.

Hospice is a federally run program, but it is regulated by each state. Therefore, the way hospice is operated in Florida is different from South Carolina. You will need to use a hospice organization in your state, and most likely, you will need to use one in your county. Your doctor can guide you through this. If you have the option of several different hospice organizations, be sure to ask your friends what recommendations they have. Not all hospice organizations offer the exact same ancillary services. For example, one organization might offer pet therapy or music therapy, while another organization might not.

All hospice organizations offer hands on medical care for your loved one. That is an extra set of eyes and hands caring for your person. They visit the person wherever they might be living (including assisted living or memory care), and they provide the medical care needed. Hospice also supplies nurses, clergy, social workers, and sitters.

Hospice is FREE to you. The costs involved are carried by the United States government and the insurance your loved one might have. Hospice also covers the cost of many medications. Once services are obtained, the organization will discuss what medications they cover and what medications they recommend discontinuing.

Let's take a moment and talk about discontinuing some medications. When we start entering the end of life, it is wise to rethink all the medications being taken to sustain or improve life. Some of these medications are causing side effects, and those side effects are being managed by yet another medication. Hospice will help identify which medications are really not necessary at this point in the caregiving journey.

Hospice also supplies (at least in most states) equipment that might be needed. This can include hospital bed, wheelchair, walker, bedside toilet, etc. These items are offered at zero cost to you.

When should your person go on hospice? The minute they qualify. An assessment is easy and done without charge. Investigate this with your doctor. That is the easiest way to get this wonderful service on-board.

CHAPTER 15

Her Last 24 Days -
Things Momma Said

This chapter is hard for me to write. It makes me sad, yet it makes me remember my sweet and crazy Momma. She was the love and light of my life. Correction – She still IS the love and light of my life. That will never change. Just because she is residing in Heaven doesn't mean anything has changed in our relationship. I just miss her more!

> "Well done, good and faithful servant! You have been faithful with a few things; I will put you in charge of many things. Come and share your master's happiness!"
> (Matthew 25:21, NIV)

The last 24 days of Momma's life were spent in the small group home she resided in. She loved it there, and I was so very happy with the care she received. I specify the last 24 days because I spent those days with her. I think I slept in my own bed two nights. The other 22 nights, I slept in the floor beside her. I knew Momma was leaving this world, and I was determined to be there when it happened. And I was!

My days were spent talking to her, and sometimes she would respond. Most often, however, I got zero response. In fact, one of the last complete sentences my Momma said to me was, "Pookie, get your ass over here." I told you she had a sense of humor. She made us both laugh.

As the days continued on, our conversations became one-sided, but then she would say something right out of the blue. Her favorite caregiver entered the room one day, and Momma said, "You were told to leave me alone." Well, OK! First words in days, and she was not happy. Such is life.

While my husband was sitting with her while I took a break, she said, "I see him. It's time for me to go. You can't go with me." He was concerned she was dying at that moment, but she had days yet to linger. We don't know who she saw. Was it Jesus? Was it her husband? Who was it?

Once Momma said, "I want it." I responded, "Momma, pray and ask The Lord for what you want." She said, "I have prayed and prayed. You don't know how much I want to go." My eyes filled with tears then, as they are while I type this. Knowing Momma was looking forward to Heaven filled me then and now with great joy.

And then there were times when she might not have been quite so spiritual. Once, right out of the blue, she said, "I don't drink beer." I was not quite sure what that was about, but OK!

The time that I remember most vividly happened just after she had gotten comfortable and began to sleep. I propped myself up in the most uncomfortable recliner on the planet, positioned my iPad, my book, and my cup in the proper places and began to work. About five minutes later Momma said, "Oh my! Oh my!" I quickly moved to her bed and actually leaned across her shoulders holding her. She went on to say, "IT IS SO BEAUTIFUL HERE! I AM GONNA LOVE LIVING HERE!" She said it with enthusiasm. I cried. I still cry thinking about that beautiful moment. What did she see? Oh, how I wish she had told me more.

Another time occurred when my husband was sitting with her. She said, "I can do this myself. I'm really trying. Praise God! Take me, please."

Sixteen days before she passed, late in the afternoon, I said, "Momma blink your eyes if you love me." She blinked! I said, "Blink your eyes if I love YOU." She closed her eyes and squeezed them shut. Then a small tear dripped from her eyes. Precious memories, for sure!

After not speaking for several days, Momma said, "We gotta get on with this program. Don't be a shit ass." A few moments later, she was quiet and spoke little for several more days. I tell you, she made me giggle!

Her last four sentences were, "It is incredibly beautiful! Honey, take me up there. I'm leaving tonight. I'm packed." I truly believe my Momma was seeing her husband, Frederick, and she was also seeing Heaven. The peace and love in my heart is multiplied by that knowledge.

I hope as you go through the last days of life with anyone you love that you will make notes. Write down the important, funny, meaningful, or even inappropriate things they say. You will enjoy looking back on those notes, just as I have done so with you.

On May 31st, hospice recommended we call the family. Everyone who possibly could gathered around my Momma. We laughed together and cried. We told stories, and we kept our eyes on Momma. At one point I looked at Momma and wondered if she had passed. I got up and touched her, and she was still with us. My two sisters had gathered to touch her, also, and there we three stood. The rest of the family gathered around, and Momma took her last breath.

I tried to feel for a pulse in her neck, but my hands were shaking so violently I could not do so. My niece is a respiratory therapist, and I asked her to feel for me. She did so and said, "Aunt Carol, Grandma fought a good fight. She has finished her race." We all were crying, and I started singing, and my sisters joined in –

"There's a sweet, sweet Spirit in this place,
And I know that it's the Spirit of the Lord.
There are sweet expressions on each face,
And I know they feel the presence of the Lord.

Sweet Holy Spirit, Sweet Heavenly Dove,
Stay right here with us, filling us with Your love.
And for these blessings, we lift our hearts in praise.
Without a doubt we'll know that we have been revived,
When we shall leave this place."

(Written by Doris Akers, 1962)

Momma immediately went to Heaven. It was soon thereafter I read the book IMAGINE HEAVEN, by John Burke. That book has forever changed how I view heaven, and I have shared it with so many people. It helped me see heaven in a way I had never pictured before. I know this, wherever Jesus is, life is good. Vera Jean Carpenter Pyatte Holder Feaster Holder is standing in the presence of her Lord. On May 31st, at 10:14 PM, He said, "Well, done Vera. Welcome home."

THANK YOU

Dear Reader –

I hope and pray this book has been meaningful, enlightening, educational, and uplifting. Your journey is not easy. However, your journey is so meaningful. Don't go it alone. Pull on the resources around you. There are so many people willing to help in various ways. You just need to ask.

I am here for you, also. Write me at carol@letstalkdementia.org. I will respond! I am happy to be the hands and feet of Jesus here on earth. We are also called to be salt and light. I want to be all those things for the over-worked and under-appreciated caregiver.

The writing of a book is work. You write, edit, edit, and edit. Did I mention edit? Then you pray the book reaches the hands of that person who needs it most. Maybe you are THAT person.

I want to thank those folks who put up with me when I am writing. Of course, my husband gets to hear updates as I work through them each day, but he should be used to all this after thirty-seven years of marriage.

My daughter, Brandie, takes time from her busy life to read and correct my manuscripts. I asked her not to tell me all my mistakes. Just fix them and move forward!

I want to thank David Longfield-Smith. I met David shortly after moving to southwest Florida at a Rotary Club meeting. He was the speaker on behalf of The Blue Zones. I attended that meeting as a back-slidden Vegan, and I left as a newly converted plant-based, whole foods, Blue Zones Project warrior. David, your words are still in my head, and my life will forever be changed because of them. THANK YOU. (Tell Madeline I miss her!)

I thank Dr. David Perlmutter, Dr. Daniel Amen, Dr. Dean Sherzai, Dr. Ayesha Sherzai, Dr. Michael Breus, Ocean Robbins, John Robbins, and Peggy Sarlin for the hours upon hours of reading and video classes you folks have produced. You continue to empower me in my journey of helping others. THANK YOU!

Blessings and smiles,

Carol Howell
www.letstalkdementia.org
carol@letstalkdementia.org

[1] Dr. Daniel Amen, MEMORY RESCUE, 2017, (Tyndale House Publishers), xix

[2] Dr. Dean Sherzai, Dr. Ayesha Sherzai, THE ALZHEIMER'S SOLUTION, 2017, (HarperCollins), 5

[3] Dr. Brooke Goldner, GREEN SMOOTHIE RECIPES TO KICK-START YOUR HEALTH & HEALING, 2013, (Express Results), vii

[4] Deby, Facty Staff, 10 Health Benefits of Omega-3, www.facty.com, Facty Health, 2/23/2021, https://facty.com/food/nutrition/10-health-benefits-of-omega-3/1/, 11/16/2021

[5] Dr. Dean Sherzai and Ayesha Sherzai, THE 30-DAY ALZHEIMER'S SOLUTION - The DEFINITIVE FOOD AND LIFESTYLE GUIDE TO PREVENTING COGNITIVE DECLINE, 2021, (HarperCollins), 205

[6] Dr. Michael Breus, THE POWER OF WHEN, 2016, (Hachette Book Group)

[7] Dr. Daniel Amen, MEMORY RESCUE, 2017, (Tyndale House Publishers) 250-251

[8] Food Revolution Network, "Living Lively Through The Power Of Plants," https://community.foodrevolution.org/products/frs21/day-4, Food Revo-

lution Network, 2021, 11/16/21

Made in the USA
Columbia, SC
19 January 2022

54230009R00063